# WORTHY

Copyright © 2019 **Shannon Evette** All rights reserved.
ISBN: 9781688058323
**Worthy Vision Publishing**

**WORTHY**

To my Three Kings. I am honored to be your mother. May you always know, embrace and *walk in* your worth.

*This book is dedicated to The One who reawakened my heart and helped me remember. Thank you.*

## Table of Contents

Why Worthy? Reflections from The Author... ..................................7

A Case for Self-Worth.................................................................. 12

Key One: Courage..........................................................................27

Key Two: Choice ........................................................................... 48

Key Three: Connections ............................................................... 66

Key Four: Compassion .................................................................. 84

Key Five: Clarity ...........................................................................107

Key Six: Character ....................................................................... 127

Key Seven: Called ........................................................................ 147

Key Eight: Complete................................................................... 167

# Why Worthy?
# Reflections from The Author...

Congratulations on making the courageous step towards healing, restoring, and reawakening your God-given value. It is the inner work of the soul that cultivates outer prosperity in life. The decision to view yourself as God does, *worthy,* creates your quantum leap into an extraordinary experience in life, purpose, and love.

**Worthy** is your freedom map; it is your guide back home. You are worthy, just as much as anyone else to create a life that reflects your highest calling. When we transform our inner being, our outer habits follow.

In the biblical story of the prodigal son, we learn of a man whose life slipped into unconsciousness. He squandered his wealth and ended up sleeping with pigs. His conditions did not reflect his Father's dream for his life, nor his own.

His poor choices reflected his compromised view of self. Like many of us, he forgot that the power to change his life was one decision away. He finally decided that *enough was enough!* He chose to leave the familiar world of his suffering and begin the brave path towards his freedom. Like the prodigal son, we may have found ourselves in situations in life that caused us to forget our worth. It often takes experiencing the depths of wallowing in pain to rise and remember that we deserve better. It took courage for him to get up from the paralysis of his poor decisions and start on the road towards accepting God's abundant grace. The scripture speaks of His Father waiting patiently to receive his son with open arms and *immediate restoration of his worth.* **(Luke 15:21-24)**

I believe the heavens await our return to our senses. When we wake up from our soul-slumber, the angels sing. Our decision to rise and take back the reigns of our life from the grips of shame, unworthiness and foolish pride, honors the God who created us.

Your past does not define you, God defines you. Culture does not define you, God defines you. Your social or relationship status does not define you, God defines you. We open our hearts now to ask the holy question: *"God, who do You say I am?"* We allow and make room for that glorious answer to reveal itself as we walk by faith.

## You Were Made for MORE!

"Let us not limit our acceptance of life by our own feelings of unworthiness. It is an insult to our Creator to say that man, God's creation, is unworthy. The most adequate and realistic self-image of all is to conceive of yourself as "made in the image of God." You cannot believe yourself made in the image of God, deeply and sincerely with full conviction, and not receive a new source of strength and power."
– Dr. Frank G. Slaughter

You may be at a sacred crossroads in your growth journey. Or perhaps you have decided that you could not continue another moment living a false identity and denying the true calling of your heart. Maybe you've reached a place of righteous rebellion against the limitations and expectations of a fallen and confused society. Or, perhaps you know it's time to simplify your life and fulfill your core purpose. Right now, something in your heart and soul is rising, remembering and recognizing that you desire and deserve more. You deserve deeper intimacy with God, more honesty and ease with yourself and more connection in purpose and love.

There are illuminating moments of clarity and courage that help to reset our entire future. These are the painful *change-it-all*-moments. These are the decisive moments of release that ensure our ability to soar higher than ever before. There are Divine moments of decision where we choose between the bridges to cross ahead of us, and those to burn behind us. Contained within our tears over the destruction, is a purification, a cleansing glow from within, guiding our glorious journey into new dimensions of purpose.

These redefining moments propel us to move out of self-created darkness and move forward into our higher destiny, guided by the light of God's truth.

We may endure years of avoidance, denying and distracting our hearts, until our day of atonement. Rebirth is a beautiful, redefining moment where we can no longer deny that our transformation will only come through surrender to a Higher calling and Source.

This journey of embracing your worthiness is an inner-revolution. We open our hearts to experience and know ourselves and our Creator in more profound ways, and we transcend our self-imposed doubts. We heal. We grow.

The cultivation of our self-concept is a process in which we consciously and proactively engage. Self-worth and self-acceptance are not auto-renewing. Daily, we choose to honor rather than reject our hearts. Everyday, we decide to embrace our value in all things. After a significant transition such as death, betrayal, divorce, or financial loss, we become more intentional and focused on the journey of self-restoration and growing in deeper intimacy with God, our Healer.

When we accept our sacred mission in life, we understand that our "**Yes**" is holy, as is our "**No.**"

Through a mission-mindset, we learn to set healthy boundaries; we guard our hearts and gather our focus. We understand that delay does not mean denial. We stop fighting against our growth and release the courage to leave our comfort zone.

We get into agreement and alignment with God. We go from living with mere sight to becoming people of VISION.

We are here on this earth to fulfill a Divine and necessary mission. Our souls are ever-evolving, co-creatively inviting the challenges in our outer life to purify our hearts and minds. Unworthiness invites unhealthy suffering. Alignment with God allows times of sorrow to produce deeper fruits of compassion, wisdom and peace within.

***Worthy*** is a personal growth method guided and ripened by God's redemptive grace.

For children of God, there is always a purpose for pain, a pearl of profound wisdom that springs from our wounds, providing a clearer understanding of grace and destiny. We are journeying into the wisdom of God, covered by the glory of unconditional love.

We are finding our way back home to tend to the soul. We understand that healing our relationship with *self* is crucial to the foundation we will bridge with God, destiny, and others.

The teachings contained in **Worthy** have been a part of my private healing practice for more than two decades. These proven methods help to reawaken, restore, and remind people of the value they already possess within. What you think of you matters, your thoughts are the filter through which every other relationship in life must flow. The words of inspired wisdom and proven spiritual strategy contained in ***Worthy*** will supercharge your God-confidence and personal power. You will rise in influence, prosperity, and inner-peace as you embrace your new identity, beliefs and behaviors based on the truth of your God-given value. You will flourish in life and thrive in love.

You will emerge after the reading and conscious application of these principles empowered to live balanced and whole.

Life is mirroring our deepest beliefs and habits back to us. Since all life is passing through the filter of self, elevating our self-concept becomes a sacred and urgent priority.

The conscious growth methods contained within ***Worthy*** will aid you in rediscovering and trusting in your truth. It all begins with you.

It's time to stop chasing validation outside ourselves. We have been taught to demand that external conditions change to ensure our happiness. Happiness and peace are *inner jobs.* We have long paid our suffering dues. Our tears have watered the garden of the seeds our faith planted. It is time for our harvest. We have gone through the purifying flames of our trials, and scripture promises us **beauty for ashes. (Isaiah 61:3)** It's time to live with freedom, openness, wholeness, and the radiance that can only shine from a life that has been through the fire. We rise like a phoenix from the ashes of necessary destruction. We release all that was false, purified by the beautiful, holy light of all that burned away. No matter what you had to go through to get here, you are still rising, still seeking, still growing, always evolving, and *still* **WORTHY.**

# A Case for Self-Worth

**SELF-WORTH MATTERS**

"You can be the most beautiful person in the world, and everybody sees light and rainbows when they look at you, but if you yourself don't know it, all of that doesn't even matter. Every second that you spend doubting your worth, every moment that you use to criticize yourself; is a second of your life wasted, is a moment of your life thrown away. It's not like you have forever, so don't waste any of your seconds, don't throw even one of your moments away."
– C. JoyBell C.

Self-worth determines our view of life, God, people, and ourselves. Our opinion of self directs the entire function of our being, thoughts, and our choices. How we openly receive the profound message of God's love, peace, and abundance depends on how we view and value ourselves. Unworthiness will propel us to chase people and things that would only harm our soul upon receipt. Disconnection from our God-given worth limits our vision. Our relationships rise and fall in the reflection of our self-value. Self-worth, based on the truth of our identity in Christ, is the foundation for every great endeavor and is the birthing ground of personal freedom.

When we suffer from low self-worth, we will resist the very opportunities that can transform our lives. Moreover, as a result, we reject the beauty of our dreams. We ignore the whispers of our deepest heart's desires. When we struggle with unworthiness, we will close ourselves to the freedom and power of open-hearted-vulnerability.

We will hide and shrink from life, never allowing ourselves the freedom to live out our dreams or connect intimately with others.

Spiritual leader, and best-selling author, Byron Katie, once described that at the lowest point of her suffering and depression, she slept on the floor, feeling unworthy to sleep in a bed. Many of us are on the floor of our own lives, refusing to rise to our calling of purpose, peace and prosperity.

You might be fighting to get back to yourself — wading through waters of loss, grief, setbacks, and uncertainty. Shattered hopes and dreams are all you have left of your positive beliefs and spiritual striving. There can be a profound mental frustration after years of religious devotion when you feel that you still lack the understanding of how to manifest your heart's desires.

So, maybe you have reached a place where you are tired of burying your head in the sand to endure another five, ten, or fifteen years to see results in your life. Maybe, just maybe, the divide between the life you envisioned and your present reality has grown so deep that you have reached a place of "divine discontentment." A place that is so profoundly painful that you are willing to roll up your sleeves, put in the work, and explore yet another realm of uncharted emotional territory. Keep reading. You're on to something.

## SELF-WORTH AND PERSONAL VALUE

> "Of all the judgments that we pass in life, none is as important as the one we pass on ourselves, for that judgment touches the very center of our existence."
> – Dr. Nathaniel Branden

Romantic relationships will not flourish to their fullest potential without both partners embracing their value, dignity, and worth. Relationships mirror our *wounds, our walls, and our worth*. When a partner in romantic love feels unworthy of love, they can become vulnerable to abuse, control, manipulation, suspicion, drama, and dysfunction. When a person undervalues their heart, they can become closed, hardened, and repress their deepest desires for meaningful love, intimacy, and soul-level connection. A lack of worth may also cause us to reject subconsciously, and view with suspicion, the messages of God's grace, unconditional love, and forgiveness. The life of an unworthy person is fear-driven. Fear destroys -- love restores. Unworthiness invites lack. Love is prosperity. When we are bound to feelings of shame and unworthiness, we will always feel as if something is missing from our lives. We will ceaselessly perform, and strive, chasing outward validation of our value, unconsciously forfeiting the balance of sacred rest and spiritual ease. We focus on *doing* rather than *being*. When we embrace our worth, we emerge whole and life rises to meet us in new and glorious ways.

## SELF-WORTH, GOD, FEAR, AND RELIGION

> "Self-worth is the key to our capacity to fulfill our God-given destiny. Rob someone of his self-worth and you will have stolen his future. The absence of self-worth is a breeding ground for every imaginable evil."
> – Dr. James B. Richards

Rigid, law-based religion and legalism have undoubtedly been one of the most destructive forces of healthy self-worth. When self-interest is exalted, and we disregard God's truth, we forfeit our only authentic Source of love, power, peace, redemption, and worthiness. When our sense of self becomes compromised by legalistic shame, we lose a level of identity that is crucial to the development of our intelligence, freedom, and well-being.

When our introduction to a loving God becomes clouded by messages of manipulation and condemnation, we begin a spiritual journey based on self-perfectionistic performance and striving. We attempt to win by "works" what has been freely given by grace.

We frame our sense of value on human-made standards of performance, rather than the totality of God's goodness.

When legalism or guilt has been our religious introduction, we come to believe that we are unworthy, that there is something inherently wrong with us. These dogmatic messages may influence us to believe in a harsh and false image of God. We may perceive God as a disappointed parent, wagging Holy fingers at us, waiting to take something away or punish our wrong-doings. These "mistakes equal punishment" messages are also commonly seen in how we parent and raise our children. Obey, conform, or be punished.

We live in a society where people are stuck in cycles of ungrieved wounds and untreated trauma. We are living in an *age of anxiety*, and many lack the tools to repair the broken relationship they have with themselves and in turn, God, their Creator.

We can turn away from the deception of this world that has kept us in bondage to lower and harmful thoughts. We can choose to renew our faith in the beauty of God's goodness, mercy, and love.

God's Spirit is as big and powerful as we allow it to be, or as limited and caged as we confine it to be. We are the channel. Until we clear the harmful religious messages that foster shame and low-self-esteem, we will compromise the revelation of God's glory being revealed through our lives.

According to the definitive and groundbreaking work of Dr. David Hawkins in his book, **Power vs. Force**, shame is the lowest, weakest level of human consciousness. Shame is incredibly destructive to our emotional and psychological health.

Shame leaves us prone to a host of developmental illnesses. Shame is what Dr. Hawkins describes as a tool of cruelty that produces a "conscious suicide." With a fear-based and legalistic perception of God, we focus on performance rather than grace. Ultimately, we become "unworthy souls" through our perception of a "harsh and disappointed God."

I have seen first-hand how countless churchgoers struggle with compromised self-esteem, religious codependency, mistrust of their thinking, and low self-worth. When people feel bad about themselves, they become more vulnerable to abuse of power and manipulation as a means of control. The more we learn to trust God's profound healing love, and the truth of the written word, the more we learn to trust the process of our wholeness journey.

## SELF-WORTH, GOD AND FEAR VS. LOVE

> "The same God who loves us as we also loves us too much to leave us as we are. Perhaps because we tend to hold on to ideas about God that reflect our own suppositions and fears, more than God's self-revelation. We reduce God to our own dimensions, ascribing to him our own reactions and responses, especially our own petty and conditional kind of love, and so end up believing in a God cast in our own image and likeness. God's love for us will ever be a mystery; unfathomable, awesome, entirely beyond human expectation."
> – Joseph Langford

As human beings, we paint God in our image, and we forget we are created to mirror His. We limit life and love through the destructive and distorting filter of unworthiness. Our sight blocks vision.

Humankind is evolving. God's glory is unfolding. Chosen souls are awakening at an unprecedented pace. We yearn to see the Kingdom of joy and peace, here on earth. We want our devotion to match our soul's unique destiny. We have a holy desire to live in the freedom that expands our faith and sets us free from man-made boxes. We are no longer content to be lectured from the pulpit as we sit silently in the pews. We know that God is something no one can fully explain; God is to be encountered and experienced. We are ready to live in Divine harmony with ourselves and our Creator.

When your initial introduction to God is one of judgment and wrath, you may struggle with a diminished view of your value.

Often the message of religion, as interpreted by man, is: The worse we feel about ourselves, the higher we are lifted in God's view. Religious legalism is a deterrent to true spiritual healing because it places an outward focus on lifestyle. The Holy Spirit desires to capture our hearts. When you renew your mind daily through the truth of God's written word, your lifestyle will organically follow. Feeling bad about yourself is not humility, it is compromised self-esteem. Humility is joyful dependence on God.

Healthy self-worth is peace; unworthiness is the pain. Scripture states that *Godly sorrow produces repentance, yet the sorrow of the world produces death.* **(2 Corinthians 7:10)** The pain of aligning with the world's agenda can only kill, steal, and destroy the truth of your identity. Godly sorrow moves our hearts to turn away from the bondage of deception and start a new season guided by the Spirit of Truth.

When we choose God's path to freedom, the loving patience of God inspires us to repent. Repentance offers unprecedented freedom! Regret keeps us wallowing in false shame, repentance is acknowledging before God, "I did it. I am sorry. I turn away from it. I will choose Your higher way."

Repentance is spiritual maintenance. It is clean closure to an open wound. It is not diminishing like regret; it is humbly liberating.

If thoughts or voices in your head are diminishing you, shaming you, accusing you, these are the lies of the enemy of your soul. These voices create anxiety. When we align with the standard of this world, we open ourselves up to deception, fear, and anxiety.

When we view our identity through the intention of our Creator, we align with wholeness and truth. We are living in a supernatural time in the realm of the Spirit, a season of miraculous revelation, restoration and Divine grace. We cannot fulfill our destiny, purpose, or truly walk in the power of love, plagued with thoughts of shame, guilt, and unworthiness. Healthy self-esteem does not make you arrogant; it merely puts you in agreement with God's evaluation of you. Accepting your God-given worth is liberty for your soul! It sets the standard for the new life you will co-create.

**Worthy** will serve to reinforce the importance of nurturing an inner-belief system, that flows from a healthy self-worth and self-esteem.

## LOVE AND FEAR CANNOT COEXIST

> "It's not about finding ways to avoid God's judgment and feeling like a failure if you don't do everything perfectly. It's about fully experiencing God's love and letting it perfect you. It's not about being somebody you are not. It's about becoming who you really are."
> –Stormie Omartian

If I find myself performing, pleasing, and striving to satisfy God through outer rules and regulations, I come up unworthy. God's **perfect love** means being complete, not mistake-free. For too long, the historical message of religion has not left enough room for God's grace, our weaknesses, flaws, or the remarkable human growth journey. Mistakes make you human, a student in this school of life. Mistakes are simply lessons learned and wisdom gained in the perfecting process.

Without healthy self-worth and esteem, we will reject the flawed beauty of people and the complex paradoxes within ourselves. How can we honor God and dishonor God's creation? We cannot embrace and reject love at the same time.

We are already made perfect, whole and complete by Love. God, our Creator, validates our worth.

Worthiness is a birthright.

Acceptance of our value fuels our power to create the habits, thoughts, and actions to serve others with greater joy and compassion.

## WORDS AND WORTHINESS

> "Words
> are powerful
> forces of nature.
>
> they are destruction.
> they are nourishment.

*Worthy*

they are flesh.
they are water.
they are flowers and bone.

they burn. they cleanse
they erase. they etch.

they can either
leave you
feeling
homeless

or brimming
with home."

-Sanober Khan

When I was a child, we sang a song: "Sticks and stones may break my bones, but names will never hurt me." Ah, if only that were true. Words have the power to hurt and heal, and they can shape our beliefs, our life experiences, and our self-esteem. If you stopped right now and asked yourself, "Where did I get my idea of self from?" Like many of us, you may determine that the voices of childhood still ring in your head as truth. Many of the words spoken came through people struggling with their insecurities, pain, and fears. These are words that may have distorted our well-being and self-esteem.

Soul-killing words of rejection have the power to take root in our souls and diminish our birthright of worthiness. Hurtful words can reprogram us to abandon our dreams. As adults, many of us find ourselves fighting against the tapes that were recorded in our subconscious long before we could discern and separate fact from fiction. In my private inner-healing clinics and workshops, I often find that many of us are still operating from the deep traumas of childhood that remain untreated and unhealed. When the wound becomes a lie, we internalize the actions of others and assign meaning and significance that does not apply. In essence, we pay debts we don't owe, and our pain becomes suffering. The journey of life gets more relaxed when we learn to separate the wound from the lie.

The reality of a snake bite is that it's not the bite that kills, but the poison that seeps into the system becoming toxic and lethal the longer it remains. It's the same with our injuries in life that become deadly threats to our sense of worthiness. The longer they linger unexamined and untreated, the more potent their poison becomes to us.

We can be a mature adult, while internally, the "tapes" that are directing our responses and reactions are the unexamined voices of a child. Growing in worthiness requires that we become radically honest. We commit to healing the wounds of our past and clearing the lies of shame attached to the injuries. We choose to break our addiction to the story and fully engage our destiny.

The wound has become a lie when we find ourselves miserable from the mental anguish of continually replaying the story. Where is our tormentor now? We have become him.

Wallowing in old pain can serve a purpose, much like victimhood, which excuses us from taking responsibility for bettering our lives. Victims always have a story. When we are devoted to the limitations of our past, we will never live the full abundance of our destiny.

We have the power to release ourselves from the mental prisons that we patrol and marshal. We are worthy of healing and restoring peace to our lives today by declaring that the past does not have to define or dictate our future.

### THE UNHOLINESS OF LOW SELF-ESTEEM

> "If my aim is to prove I am "enough" the project goes on to infinity-because the battle was already lost on the day I conceded the issue was debatable."
>
> – Dr. Nathaniel Branden

Self-esteem is a core human need. Self-esteem determines how we act and reveal ourselves in life and relationships. The essence of self-esteem is worthiness. Happiness is a function of healthy self-esteem. Self-esteem is also rooted in our belief in our ability, adequacy, or competence to handle life and deal with change. Where unworthiness might whisper, "I don't deserve it," compromised self-esteem whispers, "I can't handle it."

Self-worth is the value we possess as human beings. Self-esteem is the anchor that directs that value. The person with low self-value cannot be in a loving, healthy partnership with people, life, or themselves. When the lens we see ourselves through distorted, our quality of life is diminished.

We cannot love others with complete freedom when we suffer from low self-esteem because we process experiences through a self-centered view. We attach additional meaning to the words of others -- we take things personally, we open ourselves to paranoid thoughts, and self-accusation. We live from our triggers instead of our truth. We strive, perform, and people-please to earn our worthiness, we cannot *rest and receive.* When we are continually striving to prove our worth, we can become addicted to the approval of others. While pleasing others may help ease doubts temporarily, we eventually return to the internal thermostat of our sense of worth.

Self-esteem is different from self-worth, yet they are complementary, confirming, and cooperative states of being to one another. Self-worth is our human birthright. Self-esteem is our evaluation of self. It is how we project ourselves in the world and how life responds. Nathaniel Branden, in his definitive and classic book: **The 6 Pillars of Self-Esteem** describes it this way: *"The value of self-esteem is not merely in the fact that it allows us to feel better but that it will enable us to live better-to respond to challenges and opportunities more resourcefully and more appropriately.*

*The level of our self-esteem has profound consequences for every aspect of our existence: how we operate in the workplace, how we deal with people, how high we are likely to rise, how much we are likely to achieve, with whom we are likely to fall in love, how we interact with our spouse, children, and friends, and what level of personal happiness we attain."*

Healthy self-esteem leads to a healthy life. It aids our creativity, courage, and flexibility. Low self-esteem can be blinding, making us doormats for abuse, or can cause us to become rigid, fearful, and hostile toward others and ourselves. Our relationship with the self is the foundation of this life and what we are called to accomplish. We tend to attract people whose self-esteem mirrors our own. As we seek healthier relationships, we don't have to look much further than within. When we begin to heal and raise our self-esteem, it invites relationships into our lives that mirror this elevated view of self. All of life, love, and relationships get better when we get better.

## DON'T UNDERESTIMATE YOUR POWER TO CHANGE AND GROW

"We are not trapped or locked up in these bones. No, no. We are free to change. And love changes us. And if we can love one another, we can break open the sky."
-Walter Mosley

Everything God makes grows. We are evolving daily. We are all growing, yet we must set an intention to consciously expand. It is not a quick fix. It is a lifestyle. Give yourself credit for having the courage to face what most people fear...themselves. It is in the daily renewing of our minds in God's Word that we replenish and grow. Forming new thoughts, habits, and devotion to a daily spiritual practice will deepen our intimacy with God and make room for the miraculous.

Growth has many layers. Each day as we rise, we remove the old grave clothes of a broken identity rooted in low self-evaluation. We make a conscious choice to come up higher in our honor of ourselves and our Creator.

Our worth is a birthright. It is our task to remember and to remind ourselves when we forget our value. When our inner-voice of judgment attacks, we must not forget the truth of God's grace. When we are tempted to internalize the actions of another and take it personally, we must remind ourselves to let go. When we find ourselves striving for perfectionism through unconscious feelings of shame and fear, we must remind ourselves that we are already enough.

When we view life as a vehicle of growth, we can create opportunities through our obstacles. We do have the power, faith, and courage to transform the life we have settled for, into a life we deeply desire.

We must liberate ourselves to break the shackles that low self-esteem and unworthiness created. We are on a Divine mission, reclaiming all that we have forfeited by forgetting ourselves.

We must find the courage to stop seeking from others what we have the power to give to ourselves. When we take our soul-level question of worthiness to others; we put ourselves at the fragile mercy of people who might still be healing their self-concept. We can look within and acknowledge God's truth, or we can continue the instability of grasping outside of ourselves for validation, living disconnected from our hearts. The choice is ours. What if, instead of allowing the distorted voices of false beliefs and opinions of others to dictate our self-view, we asked God to see ourselves through the clarity of His eyes? Unlike any other creature in the universe, man can, through changing our perceptions, choose to co-create our miracles.

## DOES GOD NEED ME TO FEEL BAD ABOUT MYSELF TO PLEASE HIM?

> "The greatest commandment is that you love God with all of your being. The second is an extension of the first- that you love your neighbor as you love yourself. We do not have two commandments here, but three: to love God, to love yourself, and to love others. Jesus made it plain that self-love is the basis of proper love for a neighbor. The term self-love has a wrong connotation for some people. Whether you call it self-esteem or self-worth, it is plainly the foundation of Christian love for others. And that is the opposite of what many Christians believe."
> – David A. Seamands

God does not suffer from insecurity. We honor God when we feel good about ourselves. The gospel is called, "the good news." God's goodness is always seeking us. When we agree with God's view of us, we flow to a greater level of truth, confidence, and freedom. It takes a humble person to embrace confidence. It takes a confident person to embrace humility. God has blessed and empowered us with the covenant of unconditional love. Hiding or diminishing our gifts or talents in no way brings God glory. It requires humility to even receive a compliment without the impulse to reduce ourselves. The truth cannot be lived and denied at the same time. To reject loving the self negates the highest calling, **Love.**

Scripture states, we cannot love an unseen God and not love our brother. **(1 John 4:20-21)** What if we were the "brother" in need of love the most? We can only give from what we possess. If I am limited in self-love, I block the overflow of genuine and selfless love to others.

When we struggle with a lack of healthy self-love and self-esteem, we call unworthy what God has given priceless value. We reject what God has unconditionally accepted. We hate what God passionately loves. We question what God has already settled. We are God's hands extended on this earth. God's purposes manifest through God's people. Aligning our self-concept and deciding to get into agreement with God's vision, rather than our limited sight, is an act of bravery and faith. We must *walk worthy of this calling.*

## IT'S TIME TO RETHINK AND CHOOSE NEW BELIEFS

"Too often, we enjoy the comfort of opinion without the discomfort of thought."
– John F. Kennedy

So much of our suffering is internal, and yet we keep striving for external success, deceived into believing that what's outside of us can redeem what's within. Life is revealing our core beliefs to us through the painful circumstances and patterns that we repeat. To change what is showing up in our external lives, we must change the internal dialogue and beliefs of our hearts.

Nothing and no one is coming to save us; we must rise from the paralyzing effects of our thoughts. We must unlock the doors and set ourselves free. Suffering increases through resistance; surrendering to the process of our transformation cultivates peace. Often, without a healthy sense of self-worth, the real change our heart desires will be denied by the quick judgments and limitations of the mind. Our logical minds accept the status quo; our hearts desire more.

## TAKING PERSONAL RESPONSIBILITY FOR WHOLENESS

"Healing always involves facing truths we'd rather not face, and accepting responsibility we'd rather not accept."
– Dr. David Hawkins

**The Eight Keys** of Healthy Self-Esteem outlined in **Worthy** will challenge you to rethink and re-examine your core beliefs. **Worthy** will take you on a journey into the depths of family conditioning and past shame that has attempted to undermine your worth. **The Eight Keys** of Healthy Self-Esteem will require you to stop blaming, being a victim and falling into familiar patterns of powerlessness. You will be inspired and provided with the tools to become the champion of your dreams. No longer will you be limited by the soul-level lie of inadequacy or *not enough*.

With a proper, healthy embrace of your worthiness and self-esteem, you will be able to move forward unencumbered by the paralyzing fears of judgment, abandonment, and rejection. More importantly, you will evolve in your daily determination to love, value, and honor yourself. Your relationship with yourself will improve drastically. You will understand the value of your own self-assessment. Self-worth is the driving power for transformative change; it is the anchor for rebuilding life and experiencing lasting, holistic personal growth.

Self-worth emboldens us with the courage not only to begin but also to remain consistent on the journey of coming back home to the truth of who we are. Welcome to wholeness, sustainable change, and breathtaking freedom. Welcome to the adventure of a lifetime. Welcome to **Worthy**.

# Key One: Courage

### THE COURAGE TO WELCOME CHILDLIKE FAITH

"At what age did you conclude that wishes were merely childish things? Who told you to "grow up" and robbed you of your dreams? Let's reclaim your childhood faith in wishes, and let's take it one step further to believe in yourself. Believe that if you wish for something, it can happen. Believe that you can be the "somebody" you wished you could be. Believe that you can change something about yourself that doesn't satisfy you. When it comes to wishes, maybe it's time to stop being such a grown-up, it's time to return to that state of mind when imagination allowed you the absolute freedom to ask for the impossible, the impractical, and the inconceivable. As adults, we call it prayer, visualization, or focus. But from a childlike mindset, it's just wishing."

– Squire Rushnell

We are instructed in scripture to have the faith of a child. **(Matthew 18: 2-4)** As adults who have suffered some blows, setbacks, and heartbreaks in life, *hope* may feel like it's setting us up for more disappointment. Asking for what we genuinely desire makes us vulnerable to rejection and being let down. Trying something new opens us up to the possibility of failure. When we dare to share our dreams with others, our hearts are unmasked, naked, and our souls are exposed. It takes great courage to remove the graveyard bandages from around the deadened places of our hearts and believe again.

When we bury our heads in the sands of quiet resignation and apathy, courage beckons us back to the truth that may be hidden by oceans of regret, delays, and rejection. The desire to live with the fullness of joy will take us on a journey through lost corridors--those places where we have hidden from our desire and rejected our hearts. Courage allows us to release the need to control the outcome and trust that we are living our way into the answers. Living in alignment with God cultivates joy.

Life is big, abundant, and amazingly yielding to our most prevalent thoughts. It takes courage to loosen our self-imposed shackles and self-protective measures. It takes courage to pursue God and our dreams with childlike faith.

Faith requires a conviction. Conviction creates motion. It's cheap to critique the real players from the sidelines. It's easy to criticize what someone else dared to create, yet harder to look within and confront what we have not.

What do you desire? What would you ask for right now if you knew failure wasn't an option? What parts of your heart have you numbed to avoid future pain?

Small thinking limits life. God framed the universe and all its vastness. If we examine the beliefs of our heart, we will come to realize that frequently we play it safe, predictable, and controllable. We confine God to mental cages that mirror the limitations of our minds. Big, bold thoughts and prayers do not intimidate an Infinite, Omnipotent Creator; yet, we do limit the endless possibilities of life to the way we perceive ourselves. Self-worth sets the standard. We will receive our lowest expectation or our highest intention. The courage of vision means going beyond your reach and venturing into new territories that will stretch, expand, and unveil you.

## COURAGE REFUSES TO BE INTIMIDATED

"It's OKAY to be scared. Being scared means, you're about to do something really, really brave."
–Mandy Hale

The action we take today has the potential to move mountains. As scripture reminds us, "faith without works is dead." **(James 2:20)** It takes courage to make that call, to take the meeting, to show up in your authentic self, to write the book, to launch out into destiny.

Steve Jobs said: "Everything around you that you call life was made up by people who were no smarter than you." 'They' don't have something that you lack. It's an illusion, courtesy of your most consistent enemies - fear and resistance, playing games with your mind. Every great warrior feels fear, and every great entrepreneur knows dread. Every daring soul knows hesitation. It takes courage to rise despite these distracting feelings of inadequacy.

Courage empowers us to get out of our way. With courage, we deepen in self-respect and God-conviction. Vision requires that we put an end to fear-based, limited thinking. You are worthy of expanding in thought and faith inspired imagination. The healthier your sense of worth, the more at ease you will be while dining at the table of your destiny.

## COURAGE TO LEAVE YOUR COMFORT ZONE

"Trust only movement. Life happens at the level of events, not of words. Trust movement."
– Alfred Adler

The world's most dangerous place is our comfort zone. Even if our site of comfort has become painful, at least it is familiar, and that is why a comfort-zone can be paralyzing. Everything we desire in life is found right outside of our realm of comfort. Greatness always calls us beyond what's familiar. The reason self-worth plays such a crucial role in our manifestation of the life we desire is that we rarely rise above our worth's comfort zone.

I worked with a private client several years ago who desired a new income. She craved a new level of recognition and respect in a field in which she had put many years of hard-devoted work. She prayed for the position, wrote down her vision, and spoke it daily. When the time came to announce the big promotion, she couldn't shake the inner knowing that her time for advancement had come. She did indeed receive the position and was overjoyed!

After a few months on the job, she started complaining about the harsh treatment by her co-workers. She also seemed to be engaging in a power struggle with her new supervisor. She felt disrespected, undervalued, and not recognized for the hard work and innovation she was bringing to the organization. I asked her, "Does this mountain look familiar?" I knew she was back in her comfort zone -- a place of self-fulfilling creation. As much as she outwardly spoke that she wanted and desired change, her sense of self-worth, like a magnet, created more of the same. It was a new role, but it was the same story. Her pain had become a familiar, self-fulfilling prophecy.

During our private-coaching work together, she recognized and chose to release the negative patterns of thought. She decided to raise her intentions and feeling of expectancy through the power of biblical meditation and visualization. She expanded her view of herself, God, and life.

When our internal view of God and self expands, we discover the courage to tolerate our happiness, without the temptation to self-sabotage.

Your comfort zone may be a mentality, a neighborhood, a relationship, or a way of being that no longer reflects your genuine essence. Our fears of uncertainty keep us small, bound, and shackled to familiar places. Our heart longs to soar past all limitations. Courage ignites our hearts and unshackles our minds. When we escape our comfort zones, we are free to live in our wildest expression of truth.

**THE COURAGE TO REWRITE YOUR STORY**

> "We are all captives of a story."
> – Daniel Quinn

When you look around at your life, what patterns do you see? Painful patterns are not to be ignored but examined, uprooted, and faced. What we tolerate, we accept. What we agree with, we choose. Blame is a cycle we get caught in that diminishes our ability to rise to the occasion of our destiny. It disempowers us and discredits our strength to overcome.

I believe in the often lengthy process of personal healing and recovery. I believe in making peace with our past and removing the power it may hold in our present or future. I do not believe in getting stuck in the story, addicted to the suffering, feelings, and energetic imprints of our past pain. We can rise today from our soul-slumber. We can choose to move forward. Moving targets are harder to hit; it is forward motion, not looking back that provides peace and power.

If the old story has us, we don't have to show up fully in life. When unworthiness is running the show, we ruminate on past pain, blaming God and others for our unhappiness.

In life, we have a choice, either we tell the story, or the story tells us. If you refuse to own the lessons of your story, the pain of the story will hold you prisoner.

How long have you been telling that story? You know, the one that keeps you from showing up fully in your calling, bravely facing the requirements of your greatness and reclaiming your joy? How long have you been repeating that same old story that robs you of happiness, inner-peace, and higher clarity? When we renew our thinking by faith in God, we walk in greater mastery over old emotional triggers.

As we mature in this worthiness journey, we begin to re-frame a life based on the higher spiritual gifts of joy, peace, gratitude, and grace. We learn like Holy Alchemists how to transmute and transform old pain into a new purpose and prosperity by the thoughts we think. Transformation begins in our thought life. A real miracle is a change of mind.

You deserve to be happy. You deserve meaningful, rewarding work, and soul-level connection with other human beings who encourage you to live the truth within your heart. You are worthy of a life that reflects and embodies God's highest truth. Having the courage to rewrite the old story means we stop using emotional guilt and shame as a weapon of spiritual violence against our future legacy and present peace.

Rewriting the story means we examine the thoughts we are most addicted to -- those unexamined beliefs that assault our happiness and dignity. We pay attention to the habitual thought patterns we allow to rob ourselves of joy. Finding the courage to forgive ourselves means we stop inviting and attracting pain and punishment into our lives.

We claim others reject us, but we reject ourselves. We deny our souls the very freedom they need to flourish. When we reclaim our hearts, we decide that life is precious, time is limited, and we are worthy of living it to the fullest.

Rewriting the story requires courage because it will cause you to rise above the familiar. It's time to get new thoughts. Now is the time to tell a new story. Start singing a new song. Life is waiting for you to make your debut. God is the producer and director of your life script. You are in the starring role. Take back your authority in Christ! Resolve to keep turning the page and coming up higher in your awareness of self, and deeper intimacy with God.

## THE COURAGE TO LET GO

> "Once your past no longer has the power to define you, your future is, quite literally, yours for the taking. Every single beautiful thing you could possibly want or imagine will be yours."
> – Dan Pearce

Most of us carry a tremendous amount of emotional weight or toxic baggage from the past. When we allow the precious resources of emotional energy to become exhausted on past regrets or old resentments, we block new growth and clarity of thought.

Letting go is a powerful gift. Letting go means we are giving ourselves permission to live and enjoy the moment. We release ourselves from the prison of our own making. When we learn to let go, we learn to value and nurture our peace. We refuse to continue tolerating the emotional suffering created by resistance. Use your energy wisely: to heal, create, to expand, to release old limiting thoughts, and to evolve in your walk with God. Letting go is a daily choice. Surrendering to our inner-calling for freedom will set our captive hearts free to the joy, peace, and love we desire.

## THE COURAGE TO BE HONEST WITH YOURSELF

> "To secure ourselves against defeat lies in our own hands."
> – Sun Tzu

Your wholeness journey requires intention, resilience, persistence, and courageous self-reflection. It takes sheer bravery to make an honest assessment of your life. Are there areas of your life that are out of order? I believe in the Divine order of God. God's love orders our steps -- leading us through inner wisdom, peace confirming our alignment with Source. We cannot neglect the work within. We cannot transcend what we lack the courage to face. We only rise above the deceptions that we dare to expose by name. Personal transformation requires self-awareness. When we overcome our resistance to truth, we overcome the world.

## COURAGE TO FACE PERSONAL TRUTH

> "Most of us have far more courage than we ever dreamed we possessed."
> –Dale Carnegie

The truth often wounds you before it sets you free. In particular seasons of this human experience, we would not have been able to handle the truth. We may have been too fragile for the truth. By God's grace, truth arrives when we have the emotional capacity to face it; thus, the timeless quote: *When the student is ready, the teacher appears.* Be patient, kind and gentle with yourself as you arrive at each new level of truth. Spiritual maturity is a lifetime journey, ever-unfolding at a God-directed pace that is perfect for each individual's path.

## THE COURAGE TO LIVE YOUR AUTHENTIC TRUTH!

"That's what real love amounts to - letting a person be what he really is. Most people love you for who you pretend to be. To keep their love, you keep pretending -- performing. You get to love your pretense. It's true, we're locked in an image, an act -- and the sad thing is, people get so used to their image, they grow attached to their masks. They love their chains. They forget all about who they really are. And if you try to remind them, they hate you for it; they feel like you're trying to steal their most precious possession."
–Jim Morrison

External roles, personalities do not create our true God-given identity. Our God-centered identity is worthiness. God established our value before the foundation of time. We matter, our voices, hearts, and desires matter. There is a silent voice in many of us crying out to say: "I may not look like you, sound like you or have the same needs as you, but I MATTER!"

It requires humility to accept the gift of grace that we have already been deemed worthy to receive. Life and circumstances will present us with a logical question: *Who do you think you are?* It's wise to know the answer guided from within. Those of us who have spent life performing, pleasing, and conforming to outside influences and expectations struggle with accessing our identity. We are afraid to unveil our truth. We fear that if we share our reality and experience rejection, what would we have left? In turn, choosing to wear a suffocating mask, we deny ourselves. We have not practiced the honor of fully being at home with ourselves.

God desires our freedom and wholeness over our temporary comfort. Freedom is a gift that allows us to transcend the limiting fears of disappointing others. We don't chase happiness; we make room for it.

We let go of what we settled for to receive what we were chosen for. We release the compromise to receive the calling. To honor our God-given mission and purpose, we might disappoint a few people.

As we rise in genuine freedom, aligned with destiny, we receive the increased power of influence. We stop trying to change people from a place of insecurity, and instead, we inspire them as we continue to rise in purpose. As we evolve, we become stronger in our ability to live in liberty, transcending above the need to carry the weight of other people's opinions.

We won't lose our desire to be liked or loved, as human beings, we need psychological visibility, acknowledgment, and loving acceptance.

We all desire validation, love, acceptance, and approval from those we care for deeply. We are hard-wired for it spiritually, emotionally, and physically. No man is an island, and very few of us have platinum self-esteem. We need one another, community, and a healthy sense of belonging on this journey of life. We are expanding now into sacred confidence that compels us to follow our hearts. We are releasing the need to convince, over-explain, and apologize for who we are. We are learning to love, trust, and reverently acknowledge God's unique expression through ourselves.

As we grow in spiritual maturity, we recognize that as much as we fear the rejection and disapproval of others, we are battling a more profound battle within. Our inner-critic is the source of our pain. Vain imaginings keep us paralyzed in overthought and resistance to taking action. When we have compromised self-value, the inner-voice of self-accusation tears us down.

Silencing the voice of our inner-critic is crucial to our emotional health and well-being. The inner voice that tears down is often a byproduct of fear. It is demonic and destructive. Reject it. If you are a born again believer and know your authority in Christ, cast it down in the name of Jesus. Refuse its entry. There is no room for passivity when your thought life is under attack. Would you allow someone to come into your home and verbally abuse you? Refuse to let your inner-judge or the accusing voices of darkness to do it. It is destructive to your self-esteem and self-worth. How different would your life be if you allowed compassionate, patient, and loving thoughts to build you up, rather than allowing fear-based views to tear you down? If we cannot dwell in peace with ourselves, how can we live in harmony with others?

## WHAT YOU THINK OF YOU MATTERS

> "The worst loneliness is to not be comfortable with yourself."
> –Mark Twain

What I think of me matters, what you think of you matters. We live with ourselves. We awake with ourselves; we end our day and retire to rest with ourselves. The relationship with self is the most important relationship of all to nurture. Every relationship we engage in, including our relationship with God, passes through the filter of the self. When we are healthy, and at peace within, our relationships will mirror back this truth.

When worth rises, and falls upon the ever-changing opinions and approval of others, we place ourselves in a dangerous position of rising with the approval of others and sinking with their rejection. Riding the changing waves of external approval or rejection creates more deep-seated insecurities. Worthiness inspires us to possess a strong *inner-witness* of our value.

No matter how strong our sense of worth, we are all prone to falter in life as we internalize the responses of others. One of the most wounding hits we take to our sense of self is rejection. Unworthiness will tempt us to make rejection personal, to view it through the lens of personal inadequacy.Rejection is painful, but rejection is often a gift of redirection and protection. Rejection meets us at the intersection of time and truth. What might be right for you today may not be able to sustain your growth tomorrow. Rejection is the forced release of a person or a way of being that no longer resonates with the more excellent vision God is calling forth in and through our lives.

When the relationship with self is whole and intact, we know how to find our way back home, to the sanctuary of peace we have cultivated within. Our body is God's temple. We can be at ease, even when we're alone because we are never alone. The most powerful person in the room is at peace with God; the wealthiest person in the room is at peace within.

Living a courageous life requires being at peace with the wholeness of your own presence. Showing up in your truth, marching to the beat of your own drum, requires bravery and boldness. Doing something groundbreaking, innovative, or new involves strength. You might feel misunderstood at times for owning your essence, but the most significant rejection of all would be to betray yourself.

## WHAT DO YOU WANT?

"The indispensable first step to getting the things you want out of life is this: decide what you want."
—Ben Stein

If you do not know what you want, how will you recognize it when it reveals itself? We become afraid to speak it, afraid to admit it. We think that by holding it within, we avoid more pain. We give up on our dreams, we determine that God has abandoned us, and people have overwhelmingly disappointed us.

The truth we try to suppress doesn't go anywhere. It builds, slowly, deeply locked within, and we find ways to compensate for this imbalance. Often, we find unhealthy ways to soothe the silent cry of our souls. To heal, we release our false need to be disappointed by life and others. This mentality has kept us in an emotionally harmful loop. It's time for a new season. To move forward, we must be clear about where we are going and be honest about what we desire.

Above all in life, I desire love, purpose, and freedom. These three desires create the anchor for my choices, time, and interactions with people. The question of what you desire is not about temporal, material possessions, but rather about the deeper calling of your heart.

Sometimes, after seasons of setbacks and disappointments, it's more comfortable not to ask for what we desire. Trauma's biggest wound is not the original wound, it is the lingering distortion of the mind. Trauma distorts our view of God, people and ourselves. Life and people feel unsafe. It's too vulnerable to open our hearts, so we harden them; yet, we find no rest within until we are honest with ourselves and our Creator. As you heal, asking life and God for what you want feels like a bold move, but there is no other alternative. Shrinking away causes us to lose self-respect. When we honor the truth of God in our hearts, we gain new levels of respect for ourselves. You are worthy of leading a life that reflects honesty and truth.

## THE COURAGE TO END OUR SUFFERING

> "When we are no longer able to change a situation - we are challenged to change ourselves."
> – Viktor E. Frankl

After losing my beloved father to pancreatic cancer, I was determined to feel every ounce of pain, every moment of grief, every touch of sadness. I was equally committed not to suffer. Grief and love melt into a healing spiritual partnering where we can yield to experience the beauty and the pain of this process.

I believed in my heart that my Dad's transition from this expression of life was a fantastic gift within itself. Through my sorrow and tears, I could see a clearer vision of beauty and love perfected between my father and me.

A love where old wounds or current strains on family ties would no longer be felt or experienced. Being fully present with my father throughout his time in hospice home care was a life-changing experience. It taught me the power of the moment.

Witnessing a person leave this expression of reality helps you understand how finite you are. It also expands you to a state of infinite love that can no longer be limited by time or space. It shows you how vast you are and how no transition will ever separate you from the love of the person who has entered eternal life. When my father passed, it expanded my view of God's profound love and comfort for me. I now had a love of my father in a way that old hurts, fear, or the inability to be vulnerable, could never again hinder.

Desiring my father's attention and approval was a lifetime script for me. With his crossing, I had it, once and forever. You see, I believe that my father's view of me, in eternity, expanded. As he looked from his now perfected place of eternal power, peace, and rest, he could truly see me, all of me. His love was now perfect, and in return, so was my love.

It takes self-respect to allow ourselves to grieve and process pain. We live in a world that medicates feelings and numbs senses with avoidance and distractions. To rise above the temptation to ignore and anesthetize our own heart's cry is amazingly compassionate. We need to give ourselves the time to rest, recover, and reassess after a significant loss, transition, or change. We deserve to get better. We deserve a life free from suffering. Daily, by faith, we walk out our healing and transformation.

Courage defeats the resistance of the mind. Courage fuels the inspiration of the heart. We regain our self-respect when we step out of the shadows of fear and take risks. Tell yourself and God the truth, feel the pain, make that telephone call, write that book, have that awkward conversation.

Courage gives us the strength to be who we are called to be and do what we are called to do.

Courage is a gift. It empowers us, strengthens us, and causes us to come back home to the truth of who we already are. Through the power of God's Love, we are more than enough.

## A WORTHY Belief

"Courage gives us the power to reclaim our lives and heal our relationship with ourselves. Courage unlocks the prison doors of our minds and causes us to rise to our greatness and personal destiny."

## WORTHY Key Takeaways:

1. It takes great courage to remove the graveyard bandages from around the deadened places of our hearts so that we can hope, wish, believe, and trust again.
2. It takes courage to rise above what others may think. It's more accessible to both cheer and criticize the players from the sidelines. It takes courage to enter the playing field of life.
3. Open your heart; thinking BIG requires courage. You are worthy of new opportunities and open doors that honor the desires of your heart.
4. As scripture reminds us, "Faith without works is dead." **(James 2:20)** It takes courage to make the call, take the meeting, to write the book, to launch out into your destiny, and to show up in your authentic self.
5. Courage empowers us to get out of our way! With courage, we deepen in self-respect and self-confidence.
6. The reason self-worth plays such a crucial role in our manifestation of the life we desire is that we rarely rise above our worth's comfort zone.
7. Only when we refuse to keep tolerating "more of the same," will we access the courage to take our power back, change and leave our comfort zone.
8. We cannot heal what we lack the courage to confront. We become free after we face the truth of our pain. We rise above once we examine our limiting, negative beliefs. Personal transformation follows courage and honesty.
9. It requires courage to be honest, as the truth often deeply wounds you before it sets you free.

10. Believing in your value is an act of honoring God, your Creator.
11. Courage is a gift to ourselves. It empowers us, strengthens us, and causes us to come back home to the truth of who we already are.
12. Asking life and God for what you want is a bold move, but there is no other alternative. Shrinking away causes us to lose self-respect. When we honor the truth of our hearts, we gain new levels of respect for ourselves.

## WORTHY Soul Reflection Questions:

1. How have you allowed the fear of other people's opinions to stop you from stepping out and trying new things that would help you discover your destiny/purpose? What will you do to change this?

2. How has a lack of courage kept you confined to your comfort zone? What can and will you do to change that?

3. How have your past experiences limited you from showing up in the fullness of your power and passion in life?

4. In what ways have you allowed the fear of failure to keep you from dreaming, thinking, and living life to the fullest? What will you do to move forward?

5. In what ways has a lack of courage kept you limited and playing life safe? How will you change this?

## WORTHY Affirmation:

"I walk in courage. I am emotionally and spiritually equipped to handle whatever may come my way. Through Christ, I am more than enough."

# Key Two: Choice

"They're certainly entitled to think that, and they're entitled to full respect for their opinions... but before I can live with other folks, I've got to live with myself. The one thing that doesn't abide by majority rule is a person's conscience."
– Harper Lee

In scripture, the apostle Paul states: **"Why should someone else's consciousness determine my liberty?" (1 Corinthians 10:29)** We all must honor our personal conscious and hold fast to our convictions. We are not spectators in our lives; we are the directors of them. We must be active participants in our own lives. Conscious choice is how we design and co-create our lives.

The ability to choose is one of the most powerful gifts God has given humankind. God will never violate a person's free will. The freedom of choice, is a mirror of God's grace. Self-responsibility power. When we struggle with unworthiness, it's easier to blame God and others than it is to look within. The forfeiting of self-responsibility and self-accountability reintroduces powerlessness. Powerlessness is a killer of healthy self-esteem and self-worth. When we blame others for dissatisfaction in our lives, we fail to access our power to change. Blame blinds us to the truth. Our lives mirror our thoughts, expectations, and habits; most of all, they reflect our choices.

## BLAME STUNTS EMOTIONAL AND SPIRITUAL GROWTH

"We are taught you must blame your father, your sisters, your brothers, the school, and the teachers - but never blame yourself. It's never your fault. But it's always your fault because if you wanted to change, you're the one who has got to change."
–Katharine Hepburn

When we blame others, we abdicate what most people genuinely fear - self-responsibility and accountability. Blame keeps us stuck. Wisdom expands us and inspires change. Blame paralyzes, taking responsibility empowers motion. Motion is holy. Sitting, ruminating, and replaying scenarios in our head keeps us trapped in the patterns of fear, *overthought* and regret. Forward movement helps us increase in co-creative power. When we allow ourselves to become stuck, we may find ourselves, "waiting to be rescued," from the process of healing and making whole the poor decisions we've made in the past. The blame mentality can rob of us of the strategy and wisdom to create a better present or future. We can slip into the unconscious state of *entitlement* and lose touch with our power to improve and heal our lives through the power of choice.

The **entitlement mentality** is a killer of worth. It makes us look to others to supply and meet needs that we are wholly capable of achieving on our own.

We select our partners, we choose our jobs, we choose our friendships, and we choose our beliefs, habits, and daily actions. In many ways, life is a moment-by-moment reflection of our choices. We are not victims; we are powerful co-creators of our destiny. Life is a movie projector revealing our inner-script. We decide which players have starring roles; we determine the location, setting, and tone. We can choose at any moment to rewrite or redirect the story that is unfolding in and through us. Become aware; seek to become conscious of how your self-worth, beliefs, and choices are shaping the masterpiece that will become your life's story.

Awareness inspires self-accountability. Focused personal growth through connection to faith, intentional learning, reading, community, and deeper thinking increases confidence within. Inner-security is the key to gently releasing the chronic patterns of suffering, blame, and victimhood.

We will engage with life in a more fulfilling and satisfying way when we embrace the power of choice. Taking responsibility for the life we are co-creating through actions and attitudes, strengthens our self-respect and confidence. When we take responsibility for our lives, we overcome the paralyzing mentality of entitlement. It is the beginning of the truth as it compels us to rise to the challenge of looking within. We have unlimited inner resources of spiritual wisdom. When we align with God's truth, we access Infinite Intelligence. As we expand in knowledge, our lives expand in ways that will far exceed our imagination.

## REDISCOVERING THE SOUND OF YOUR VOICE

> "I prefer to be true to myself, even at the hazard of incurring the ridicule of others, rather than to be false, and to incur my abhorrence."
> –Frederick Douglass

If we're not careful, our thoughts can come to reflect the recycled opinions of everyone else. We live in a conformity based culture that does not always encourage or celebrate truth. If you are to be a courageous seeker of truth, you must tune out the noise of cultural distraction and tune into the spirit of destiny. Unlearning is the key to self-discovery.

It's natural to desire the approval of others, but what does it cost you? Freedom? Peace? Self-respect? Count the cost. Is the price too high? One of the things I love about mature people, individuals who have seen some seasons of life, is that they have rediscovered the sound of their voice. Maturity allows you to live a life that is an authentic, unapologetic expression of your truth. God does not require conformity. Love inspires unique and truthful expression. God *is* love.

## IT'S BETWEEN YOU AND GOD, NOT "THEM"

> "For you see, in the end, it is between you and God. It was never between you and them anyway."
> –Mother Teresa

We often make choices in life with an imaginary counsel of "they" controlling the way we dress, live, think, and decide. The individual path is exactly that, individual. We bow down to the false idol of fearing people and forfeit the power of God, our Source. The fear of people's opinions, the inner-tyranny of thoughts we allow to plague, control, and limit our vision, voice, and value serve no one.

What kind of life are you choosing? Is it your own? We play it safe to avoid rejection and abandonment that we fear will come from others. If I am simply a by-product of someone else's thoughts and opinions, my life becomes a reflection of someone else's ideas and not my own. If I am living in a constant reactionary state to what other people *think*, how will I ever *own* my freedom?

What if we stopped to acknowledge that a large part of our lives reflect the words, thoughts, opinions, fears, beliefs, and traditions of others?

When we choose to think, question, study, reflect, and ponder for ourselves, we courageously examine all previously held beliefs. By choosing to investigate past and current views, we may threaten the reigns of long-established religious traditions, socio-economic, political, and cultural expectations. Conscious learning first requires *unlearning*. We cannot powerfully own a truth that we are unwilling to question, examine, and embrace as a function of our own free will.

This process inspires a soul-level reawakening. When it's all said and done, there is no more excellent gift than to know I will have done it *my way*. The balance of this independence is that my steps are Divinely directed. I desire to live with a reverent and obedient heart to God. In all things. Even the choice to surrender daily to God's higher calling and the leading of the Holy Spirit is *my* choice to make. Liberated people know that freedom is a gift that costs. We refuse to bow down to the false idol and addiction of pleasing people. We ignite the bravery to live our truth. The careful maintenance and development of our inner strength, against the grain of what people may perceive or think, will anger some and possibly confuse others. Our role is not to carry the burden of their opinions, but rather to make sure we are growing in alignment with destiny and self-respect.

Justifying, reasoning, or over-explaining ourselves is a sign of unworthiness. When we are at rest in our hearts, no long, drawn-out explanation is necessary. We trust our ability to say *yes* as much as we believe in our right to say *no*.

We release the fear-based need to secure the approval of others at the cost of our own. I learned long ago to stop the compulsive need to offer up reasons, justifications, and explanations for my actions. As scripture says, **Let your yes be yes, and your no be no. (Matthew 5:37)** When you are mission-minded, your "no" is holy. When you say no, you are also saying yes. Saying no to something not desired, is saying "yes" to what is. *No* is a holy and honest word that enhances self-respect and protects focused vision and purpose. We have a birthright to choose a life that reflects our values and authentic desires.

## CHOICE--- THE POWER TO CO-CREATE OUR LIVES

"We are not victims of our biology or circumstances. How we react to the events and circumstances of life can have an enormous impact on our mental and even physical health. As we think, we change the physical nature of our brain. As we consciously direct our thinking, we can weed out toxic patterns of thinking and replace them with healthy thoughts. New thought networks grow. We increase our intelligence and bring healing to our brains, minds, and physical bodies. It all starts in the realm of the mind, with our ability to think and choose— the most powerful thing in the universe after God, and indeed, fashioned after God."
–Dr. Caroline Leaf

Our minds are powerful. We have free will and free choice. Those two abilities make us co-creators of our lives. We can change, heal, and renew our minds. Scripture states: "you shall have what you say." **(Mark 11:23)**

Our words co-create our reality. We must learn to discipline our words, mind, and bodies to align with what we desire. As the wise sages say: *The body makes for a beautiful servant, but a terrible master.*

Empowered by faith, we are free to speak faith over fear; we can choose to speak gratitude rather than the language of suffering. We are the gatekeepers of our soul; we are the guards of our mental state. We decide which thoughts enter and what ideas can remain. We are not the victims of our thoughts; we are the originators and hosts of them. Our thoughts often create or prolong suffering. Our words are powerful tools of creation. A view can be changed instantly, and at any moment, we can choose to end our addiction to the pain. A heart at rest creates a mind and body at ease.

While it is true that our thoughts and deepest held beliefs determine and direct our reality, we realize that there are things in life outside of our realm of control. God is sovereign. Life is full of unfathomable mysteries. We are not omnipotent or all-knowing. Circumstances happen all the time -- natural events, tragedies, losses, and disasters. We don't control all of life. We do have the power to choose our words, beliefs, and behaviors. It is also essential to leave room for grace, Gods' loving, and redemptive flow towards us. Grace transcends human understanding, mistakes or expectations.

## CHOOSING FREEDOM WITHIN

> "Integrity is telling myself the truth. And honesty is telling the truth to other people."
> –Spencer Johnson

Honesty begins with self. Privately. Alone. When you are in moments of solitude, how do you speak to yourself? Integrity means a sound foundation. Designing a vibrant life requires a sound foundation within. What is your inner-voice? Do you constantly ruminate over past offenses and pain? Are your thoughts undisciplined, unruly, and harmful to their host? Being gracious with ourselves provides us with greater confidence to share our hearts with others. Our outer lives and relationships are the constant mirror to our inward-state of being.

Outward success follows inner peace of mind. You can master your emotions and retrain your thinking. You can cultivate an inner sanctuary that invites peace, calm, and soul-ease. You can redirect your thinking. You can overcome feelings of shame, fear, and self-doubt. You can choose to recreate your life's story. You can rise above self-inflicted limitations.

You don't have to be a victim of circumstance. You don't have to be controlled by the demands and expectations of others. You don't have to have a heart ruled by fear, depression, and anxiety. You don't have to waste away precious, countless hours in your head, over-thinking and plagued with future worries. You can, by faith and the renewing of your mind, co-create an existence of calm, peace, love, joy, and flow. It's a daily choice – it is your choice.

When you choose to liberate your mind through the practice of your faith, you open your heart to all the abundance life has for you. Embracing the power of choice is like being given the keys to the Kingdom. We are hard-wired for success, peace, joy, and freedom. The setbacks, pain, and habitual patterns of thinking reprogram us for the struggle. God lives within. Grace is a gift. God's grace is not to be strived for and earned through legalism and fear, but to be received in joy.

We can stop the recycled patterns of addictive, negative thinking, and we can make new choices to create a life that genuinely reflects our design. We have the power to both choose and receive God's abundance, wellness, sanity, and joy.

Negative thoughts are addictive. They are habitual. But, like any other bad habit, they can be replaced with something healthier and more beneficial to our emotional well-being. Decide to re-master your thinking. Refuse to let imagination and fearful worries steal your joy. Reclaim ownership of your freedom and your future possibilities.

## THE CHOICE TO MAKE SOMETHING MEANINGFUL OR SIGNIFICANT

> "If you're alone in a room and you're suffering, eventually it will dawn on you that you're the one who's causing it. Checkmate."
> –Byron Katie

How is it that one person can suffer a tragedy of epic proportions, such as sexual trauma, death or loss of everything in a natural disaster; yet, they find the strength, courage, and resilience to rebuild their lives, while another person can remain stuck in a petty offense for years? We alone assign meaning to the events that occur in our lives. Through our thinking, we decide what is significant and what is not. We choose the weight, power, and impact of the event through the meaning we assign it.

When we struggle with unworthiness, we tend to assign more weight, suspicion, and accusation to experiences with people and life. We take things personally rather than live within the freedom of detached observance. Unworthiness prompts us to become harsh judges in our lives rather than gentle observers. Judgment wounds the host and recipient of the energy. Observation allows us to examine life without internalizing everything from a small and self-centered view. Non-judgemental observance of life and experiences are the pathways of peace, higher learning, and clarity of thought.

Our thoughts and choices create more ideas and opportunities. Many people remain trapped in a cycle of unhappiness or suffering for years only by choosing more of the same thoughts. When we dwell in the past or recycle painful feelings, we are aligning with deception and attracting living proof of our beliefs, through relationships, finances, and life circumstances.

Gratitude and appreciation replenish our energy. The higher we go and grow in gratitude consciousness, the more natural and more bountiful life flows.

Daily, we are creating new, ingrained beliefs about ourselves, God, and the world around us. In the same way that we can create suffering, we can create joy. We have the right and the free will to choose our response to life. We are not a victim of anything except our lack of self-respect and understanding. Our minds need cleansing and purification as often as our physical bodies do.

## THE CHOICE TO SELF-SURRENDER

"The greatness of a man's power is the measure of his surrender."
–William Booth

The self (what we believe, love, fear, hate, honor, value, think) is continually evolving. The more invested we are in the rigid positions of the old self, the more struggle and pain we may suffer. Fear is rigid and inflexible.

Humility is relaxed, open and teachable.

For many, even the word surrender evokes a sense of powerlessness; yet, surrender to God's love is the beginning of real victory. It is coming to the end of our limitations to access the limitlessness of God. It is ending the struggle of over-thinking and welcoming the beauty of the Holy Spirit's guidance. It is giving up the resistance to life by accepting and loving *what is*. It is the ability to flow and live in the power of each moment.

Surrender is forfeiting the need to force and control life. You learn to trust Divine serendipity, flow, and alignment. Surrender is a position of the heart that invites Divine intervention. Through the power of surrender, we come to the end of our attempts to bargain, save, and rescue ourselves. We transcend the fear-based survival mode, and we begin to live with the anointing of ease. Surrender is a self-liberating choice.

Self, when driven by fear-based ego, is typically out to prove, defend, and protect. I will never forget the first time I read the scripture: *"To find your life, you must first lose it."* The first time I read it, I rejected it with all the fullness of self that I could muster. Blinded and unable to see that this was not an invitation to death, but a liberated life. I was being invited to take the journey of my

Lord Jesus -- first to the cross, then to the throne. As human beings, we often want the throne without the pain, inconvenience, or exposure of the cross. It is the crosses we endure in life that powerfully position and secure our *crowns*.

Detachment is peace. When we stop living in fear of death, we can truly live. When we are not mentally obsessed with the fear of people betraying, abandoning, or rejecting us, we experience genuine connection. When we release the desperate need for people's approval, approval comes freely. When we stop chasing love, love seeks us. Release empowers us to receive. You are worthy of feeling and living better. Know your value in all things.

## THE CHOICE TO BE HAPPY

"When I was five years old, my mother always told me that happiness was the key to life. When I went to school, they asked me what I wanted to be when I grew up. I wrote down 'happy.' They told me I didn't understand the assignment, and I told them they didn't understand life."
– John Lennon

You are worthy of happiness! Happiness, like peace, is an inside job. We must cultivate happiness daily. With each moment, we participate in the creation of our bliss. We must be devoted, committed, and persistent about nurturing an inner world that manifests in outer happiness. Not all satisfaction is internal. I do believe in the power of the environment. I feel happy in a freshly cleaned house, or sitting at the beach; it is a byproduct of God's abundant beauty made manifest by the ocean. I feel so glad when I sip hot, creamy coffee; that is self-satisfaction. I feel happy when I'm laughing with a good friend, reading a thought-provoking book, blasting music and dancing all by myself, playing with my wild and rowdy yellow Labrador "Waffles," cracking jokes and having fun with my three boys or celebrating life with my amazing community of friends! Happiness is intentional. There are habitual thought patterns that rob us of joy. Pay close attention to your moods, and the habits and the thoughts that attempt to steal happiness at the moment. When we struggle with false guilt and unworthiness, we may not even feel deserving of genuine contentment. We may have made unconscious bonds with old trauma that causes us to reject joy.

When we live from the center of personal wholeness, we give a great gift to ourselves and those we love. Wholeness attracts and cultivates everything good.

For too long, the deep, intellectual thinkers have dismissed happiness as a virtue of the silly, shallow or intellectually weak - those not deep enough to understand the complexities of the human existence. On the contrary, a happy person is the perfect picture of strength and resilience. Each day, happy people face dilemmas and the same concerns many of us face, yet, they make a choice to value and cherish personal freedom happiness creates.

Emotions are teachers. We certainly won't always feel happy. Life is Divine and messy, but that doesn't mean happiness cannot be cultivated and deeply experienced as a way of life.

Worthiness, at its core level, believes that we have a God-given right to live an abundant and fulfilling life. You've already proven you can suffer. You've more than paid your sorrow and sadness dues; so, try something different. Permit yourself to be happy. Refuse to tolerate the habitual, addictive thoughts that rob you of joy. Expect happiness and abundance and do everything in your power to choose, create, and cultivate the life you desire.

## A WORTHY Belief

*"Choice is the most powerful gift God gave humankind. Through the power of choice, we shape our lives and co-create our destiny."*

## **WORTHY Key Takeaways:**

1. Choices are how we design and co-create our lives. We are not guests in our lives; we are the owners of them.
2. We are not spectators in our lives; we are the directors of them. We must be active participants in our own lives.
3. When we blame God, or others, we abdicate what most people genuinely fear -- self-responsibility.
4. Life is a daily reflection of our choices. We are not victims; we are powerful co-creators of our destiny.
5. We cannot correctly own a truth that we are unwilling to question, dissect, and return to as a function of our own free will.
6. Our role is not to carry the burden of opinions from others, but rather to make sure we are growing in our view and respect of self.
7. We have a right to choose a life that is a reflection of our self-love, core values, and desires.
8. Our minds are powerful. The only thing in this universe more powerful than our souls is God.
9. We decide which thoughts enter our consciousness and which ideas are allowed to remain. We are not victims of our thoughts; we are the owners and originators of them.
10. Outward success follows inner peace of mind.
11. In the same way, we can create suffering; we can create joy. We have the birthright and the free will to choose how we respond to life.
12. We have the power to heal our lives, retrain our thoughts, and redesign our choices to create a life of freedom and happiness.

## WORTHY Soul Reflection Questions:

1. How has the victim/blame mentality hindered you from taking full ownership over your life? Why are you ready to change this?

2. In what ways have you accepted and tolerated less than God's best in your life? How will you change that?

3. How have you settled for a life that has just happened, rather than designing your own life? What must you do to heal this?

4. In what ways can you begin making choices that honor your true desires rather than the expectations of others?

5. What choices will you make this week, to begin cultivating personal happiness and joy?

**WORTHY Affirmation:**

"I choose thoughts, actions, and beliefs that honor my heart. Through choice, I have the power to create a life that is in alignment with love, passion, integrity, abundance, and personal dignity."

# Key Three: Connections

**WORTHINESS SETS THE STANDARD OF ATTRACTION**

"We do not attract that which we want; we attract that which we are."
– James Allen

Of all the joy and pain we encounter in life, nothing comes close to our relationships. Relationships are teachers. They reveal our hurt, our unhealed wounds, and our capacity to love, and offer grace and forgiveness. Our deepest needs as human beings center on our need for genuine love and meaningful connection. It is our most intimate relationships that penetrate our hearts, souls, and minds like nothing else in this world. When it comes to romantic relationships, nurturing a healthy self-concept is crucial. Nurturing intimacy with God and ourselves is vital to expanding our ability to connect in healthy intimacy with another human being. I once heard it said that we choose a mate who mirrors our self-esteem at the time. The person who is open-heartedly committed to growth will typically attract a person who reflects their perception of self.

**SELF-WORTH, EXPECTATIONS AND ROMANTIC LOVE**

"We cannot think of being acceptable to others until we have first proven acceptable to ourselves."
– Malcolm X

We are already loved and approved. We are already whole and complete. Instead of seeking love, we are invited to **embody** love. Become love. When we expand our sense of value, self-respect, and self-love, we enter our relationships from the overflow of strength and love, not the deficit of lack and need. When we have settled our soul-level questions of purpose and worthiness, we don't hold our partner to high, unrealistic standards. In healthy, mature love, we choose a partner based on authentic connection, passion, love, and purpose, not on meeting our temporary emotional needs. We don't attempt to change them, we humbly submit to God, to *change us*. All of life and all of our relationships better as we do.

The healthier we are in emotional well-being, the less likely we are to choose an unsafe relationship that only reinforces old wounds and old pain. In healthy, life-giving, soul-connections, our partner becomes a source of healing as their love provides a safe place for us to serve, flourish, evolve, and expand. When our partner spiritually *sees* us, affirms us, and accepts us for who we are, we **thrive**. In mature, romantic love, we must be open and emotionally mature enough to offer to a relationship that we desire to receive. It is the *giving* of service and love that heals us; it is the selflessness of love that unveils the more profound beauty of our souls. We love beyond this world's selfish, low-self-esteem-driven, "*meet my needs*," mentality, we love our mates as *unto God*. We allow our hearts to expand in grace as we first extend it. We refuse to wallow in the pain of anger, discontentment and the practice of bitterness. We gather our continual joy from a perfect Source, not from a flawed partner. We refuse to be swayed by a confused culture's ever-changing opinion of love. We lean on and seek God's wisdom regarding the biblical requirement of marriage and love; this timeless wisdom reveals all truth. We set the tone of love with our mate through humility. Seeking to serve rather than be served. The biblical law of sowing and reaping is strong in romantic love, what we offer, we receive, maybe not directly from our mates, but God is faithful. You cannot bless your mate, without blessing yourself. The peace that flows through you to them is *yours to own*. The grace that flows through you to them is *yours to experience*. The love that flows through you to your partner is *yours to embrace*. The God-surrendered relationship can be heaven on earth, a reflection of the Kingdom. An extraordinary love is experiencing our worthiness through the eyes of another.

## GENUINE ROMANTIC LOVE REQUIRES SURRENDER

> "Always say, "yes" to the present moment. What could be more futile, more insane than to create inner resistance to what already is? What could be more insane than to oppose life itself, which is now and always now? Surrender to what is. Say, "Yes" to life -- and see how life suddenly starts working for you rather than against you."
> – Eckhart Tolle

Transformational love requires openness; it requires our courageous *yes* to the present moment. It's not easy to remain vulnerable and open to love when you've suffered the heartbreak of betrayal. How do we keep our hearts open, yet guarded? Love requires the freedom of openness and the wisdom of discernment. The vulnerability may feel as if love is breaking our hearts to open them. The freedom to love is not about the object of our desire, but the personal peace and confidence provided when we choose to live authentically from the heart. God's love is the safest hiding place for our hearts as we learn how to trust again. God's love is the most reliable hiding place for a broken heart to mend.

When we surrender our desire to be in a loving romantic partnership to God, we place our trust in the Source of Love itself, not a specific person. Many of us have broken another person's heart intentionally or unintentionally. We may have caused pain while we were growing and learning how to love.

Grace is needed as we grow into love. If we need another person to be perfect or mistake-free before we can accept them, we are not ready for love. Love is the supreme teacher, and we are all yet flawed students.

To flow through life with an open and free heart positions us to attract higher love. Love attracts more love. Open hearts draw open hearts. **Deep calls unto deep**. If you want profound, extraordinary love, surrender your past fears and your future worries to God and choose to remain courageously open. Love requires nothing less.

## OUR DEEPEST HUMAN NEED IS FOR LOVE

> "There's nothing more powerful than walking in love."
> – Joyce Meyer

Distractions will never quiet our soul's longing for its highest destiny, which is love. No matter how hard we may try to pretend, no matter how cynical we are tempted to become, love will never cease calling. It is our God given purpose and design. The desire for love will never stop. Only when we find the boldness, courage, and fearlessness to surrender to all the possibilities that love holds, do we experience soul liberty. We are better in love, better when receiving love, better when giving love.

## HEALTHY ROMANTIC LOVE

> "Two is better than one."
> – Ecclesiastes 4:9

Statistics prove that people in committed, long-term romantic relationships are emotionally happier and physically healthier than their single counterparts. Many of us experienced less than loving, healthy homes. The words, *dysfunctional family*, might describe the childhood experience of a large majority of adults walking around today. People we enter into relationships with might be those who have experienced both emotional wounding and trauma. If you desire healthy love, the best gift you can give to yourself and your partner is your ongoing commitment to nurturing your wholeness. When our self-esteem is intact, when our self-appraisal is healthy and robust, we attract and sustain healthy relationships. It is through a conscious open-heartedness and a daily decision to **surrender to God's love** that we invite and expand all good things.

## WORTHINESS AND INTIMACY

"Love is patient and kind; love is deliberate. Love is seeing the darkness in another person and defying the impulse to jump ship."
– David Davenport

Intimacy means: *into me, you see.* The fear of intimacy is a fear of future perceived loss. When shame is driving the seat of the soul, we fear exposure; we fear the risk of being rejected, misunderstood, or worst of all, abandoned. Human beings are hard-wired to fear loss. If we hide our true selves and refuse to show up in our relationships with honest hearts, we lose anyway. We lose self-respect. We lose courage. We miss out on the opportunity to share something profound with another human being--our true self.

Love creates a safe place for two people to expose their truth without feeling punished, judged, or threatened by unrealistic expectations and demands. We hold sacred space that inspires our partners to shed the need to protect or prove themselves. The private world of two lovers must feel safe for them to flourish.

## WHEN IT'S TIME TO CUT TIES

"The very nature of a good relationship is how much it encourages optimal intellectual, emotional, and spiritual growth. So, if a relationship becomes destructive, endangers our human dignity, prevents us from growing, continually depresses and demoralizes us -- and we have done everything we can to prevent its failure, then, unless we are masochists and enjoy misery, we must eventually terminate it."
– Leo Buscaglia, Ph.D.

Relationships are teachers; they unveil and unbind our hearts. We all need large doses of grace and forgiveness to navigate through this life. Authentic love does not abandon people because of tough seasons or difficult times. Love is patient. For love to be powerful, it must also be wise. There are cases when a relationship has become unsafe to our physical, emotional or spiritual well being. We cannot control others; we can protect the sacredness of our own space. The beauty of inner-freedom is maintained as we exercise Godly discernment in the realm of relationships. If you are in a marriage covenant, a sacred vow, this cannot be taken lightly. Seek God; trust the leading of the Holy Spirit confirmed by the written word and seek wise counsel in those you trust.

You can love people from a distance that is safe enough for your healing and recovery. When relationship patterns become detrimental to our wellbeing, creating distance is the wisest and most loving choice to make.

Healthy relationship boundaries are a byproduct of healthy self-worth and wisdom. Relationships can be either destiny or distraction. Know that even the relationships that seemed to be one big, painful distraction offer up valuable insights for the soul that is growing and open to receive the lesson.

## DO YOUR RELATIONSHIPS MAKE YOU HAPPY OR HOLY?

"In my early professional years, I was asking the question: How can I treat, or cure, or change this person? Now I would phrase the question in this way: How can I provide a relationship which this person may use for his own personal growth?"
-Carl Rogers

Those of us who are growing in spiritual maturity understand that relationships serve as our most important personal growth tools. Through tears, we become tender. Through conflicts, we reach a deeper state of compassion and understanding of one another.

Old relationships are cleansed and reset when our minds are open to forgiveness and compassion. What if that relationship was meant to make you **holy** and not just happy? What if the mirror of that person was here to remind you of how to love more deeply, selflessly, or with greater compassion, patience, and forgiveness?

Look within, pray, and seek wisdom. The answers you seek regarding your relationship are making their way to you now. Ask God,

"How would you have me pray for this person? Love this person in a way that honors you?

Everything we need to navigate through our relationships is found within God's word and established through wise counsel. Love is not here merely to meet our needs but to challenge and grow us into a more significant and beautifully courageous version of ourselves.

## HOW OLD WOUNDS SABOTAGE NEW LOVE

> "Today, expect something good to happen to you no matter what occurred yesterday. Realize the past no longer holds you captive. It can only continue to hurt you if you hold on to it. Let the past go. A simply abundant world awaits."
> –Sarah Ban Breathnach

Whole relationships require whole thinking. When we bring old baggage into new relationships, we distort our ability to *give* and *receive* love. These unhealed wounds often turn into self-sabotage and inflict unnecessary pain on us, as well as others. It's not fair to punish a new person for betrayal and emotional crimes that occurred before their time. The best gift you can give your future relationships is healthy and more liberated you!

When we are touchy, sensitive, and easily triggered, assigning profound meaning and significance to the slightest infractions, we are not free. Being emotionally triggered and easily offended in our relationships, is a sign of an unhealed heart. A season of solitude, stillness, and restoration after heartbreak is incredibly wise.

Maturity teaches us to give ourselves the time to heal so that we don't inflict unnecessary pain upon others. We maximize the chances of attracting and nurturing healthy love when we care for our soul first. We can enter our relationships from a place of wholeness, intimacy with God, and self-respect that completes us.

## DON'T TAKE IT PERSONALLY

> "Whatever happens around you, don't take it personally... Nothing other people do is because of you. It is because of themselves. All people live in their own dream, in their own mind; they are in a completely different world from the one we live in. When we take something personally, we assume that they know what is in our world, and we try to impose our world on their world."
>
> "Even when a situation seems so personal, even if others insult you directly, it has nothing to do with you. What they say, what they do, and the opinions they give are according to the agreements they have in their own minds..."
>
> – Don Miguel Ruiz

We can misinterpret truth and meaning in communication. Our minds can mislead us. Our thoughts can be wrong when we are in judgment of another person. Quick conclusions, based on old triggers rather than heart reflection, wound the people we love and us. When we release the need to take everything personally, we relax and learn to trust the unknown. We recognize the deceitful voice of fear as it introduces panic and anxiety. Patience is essential in learning how to love -- and it starts when we have patience with ourselves first.

As we courageously grow into the maturity love requires, we learn the art of grace. The very people we blame for wounding us also made us stronger and more compassionate. The people we think rejected us are signaling to our souls that our work in this relationship is complete. The people we have hurt or disappointed offer us a mirror to purify our hearts; to forgive ourselves and to show ourselves compassion and grace on the journey.

God is wholeness. There are two sides, two dimensions to every story. If we flow in the truth of balance and the nature of wholeness, we know that for each tear we have shed, there will be laughter. For every night we've spent worried, in pain, sorrow, or heartbreak, we will be restored equally with moments of peace, passion, and joy. We have a choice. We cannot avoid pain or outrun our lessons; they are the gifts that allow us to love more profoundly, more courageously, and more selflessly.

Each one of us has a path, a sacred journey that is uniquely tied to our destiny here on earth. Relationships are the tools, mirrors, and, often, even weapons used to sharpen and reveal us. Just as our path is personal, so is the growth journey of the person we have chosen to love. When we refuse to internalize another person's struggle and ask instead, "God, what am I here to learn?" "How do I love this person in a way that honors their design and your purpose?" We can move forward with a new level of peace, clarity, and understanding.

## HEALTHY SELF-WORTH AND AUTHENTIC COMMUNICATION

> "Most of us avoid telling the truth because it's uncomfortable. We're afraid of the consequences--making others feel uncomfortable, hurting their feelings or risking their anger. And yet, when we don't tell the truth, and others don't tell us the truth, we can't deal with matters from a basis in reality."
> –Jack Canfield

Love requires courage and maturity. Mature, healthy love is a safe place to share the depths and complexity of our hearts.

Authentic relationships require gut-level communication, openness, and honesty. When we repress our true feelings, they don't go anywhere. They are buried alive. Studies have long documented the connection between physical illness and repressed emotions. Your body will act out what your heart refuses to speak out. Or, like the steam from a kettle, repressed emotions will eventually reach a boiling point and then boom! Finding the courage to be honest now is better than inflicting more damage later.

When we deny ourselves the freedom to share from our hearts, the other person in the relationship suffers as well. How can we grow, heal, and expand in our relationships if we don't engage in honest, open communication? If I cannot be emotionally naked and unashamed with you, we cannot grow together.

The best relationships are ones where both people are committed to honesty, communication, and openness; where issues are dealt with lovingly and quickly. When repressed emotions fester, they cause a subtle emotional divorce. We lose sight of the primary feeling -- things become cloudy; we miss opportunities for authentic growth and more profound connection through grace and understanding. Remember, the next time you convince yourself that you are "keeping the peace" by silencing, avoiding or repressing your emotions -- this peace is false. True peace comes with compassionate honesty and wise communication.

## WORTHINESS AND AUTHENTICITY

"Relationships are ultimately us meeting ourselves through another."
— Susan Winter

When we flow in relaxed authenticity, we invite our partner to flow in their freedom as a reflection of our own. Our transparent courage may serve to inspire the same bravery in our mates. Relationships are soul mirrors.

Choose the person with a safe heart that allows you to feel at ease and open in their presence. Choose the person worthy of your trust in the areas you need to trust them the most. When people have shown themselves worthy of our vulnerability, we can begin to reveal the layers, the complexity, the beautiful colors, and the uniqueness of who we are. Love requires the courage of openness and transparency. When we guard ourselves to protect ourselves from pain, we also block joy and love. Fear and resistance diminish who we are. Love introduces us to the most excellent versions of who we are. People come into our lives to help us reveal layers within our hearts that we wouldn't have the capacity to see without them. Love evolves us.

## SELF-WORTH AND ROMANTIC LOVE

"You never lose by loving. You always lose by holding back."
– Barbara De Angelis

We were created by God to love and be loved. We are not sappy or weak for desiring to be visible and valued by another human being. Healthy, romantic love serves as a confirmation and spiritual validation of our worth through the eyes of another.

We are at our absolute human best when we are giving and receiving love. Being valued, cared for, adored, and cherished by another human being reinforces and strengthens our feelings of inner security.

Giving love, serving another human being, loving someone through difficult times, being there for someone we love, introduces us to a higher part of ourselves. When we know that someone is genuinely there for us, our soul exhales. We rest within our hearts. Learning to love another human being is the most excellent tool for personal growth. When choosing a life partner, don't merely look at outward things: job titles, material possessions, and looks. All these things are subject to change. Choose the person who is the safest place for your heart.

Choose the person who inspires you to open more fully, grow spiritually, and to love with deeper abandon. Choose the person God has called you to serve in passionate love and grace. Choose the person who believes in you. Choose the person who is mature enough to handle all of what you bring to the table. Choose the person worthy of your heart, and then do *everything* in your power to humbly grow, heal, and evolve in Christ to be *worthy* of theirs.

### A WORTHY Belief

"Relationships are our greatest source of wealth. Healthy love and meaningful connections are essential to our joy, spiritual growth, and emotional well-being."

## WORTHY Key Takeaways:

1. Of all the joy and pain we encounter in life, nothing comes close to our relationships. Relationships are our most excellent teachers.
2. People withhold love because they fear abandonment, but surrender calls us to abandon our fears and fully love.
3. To connect with another human being on an intimate, soul level is our heart's deepest yearning.
4. Only when we find the boldness, courage, and fearlessness to surrender to all the possibilities that love holds, do we experience soul liberty.
5. It is not needy or desperate to desire romantic love; it is wise.
6. It is through a conscious open-heartedness and a daily decision to **surrender to love** that we attract and expand all good things.
7. When we take old baggage into new relationships, we distort our ability to receive and give love and truth.
8. Love requires courage and maturity. Mature, healthy love should always be a safe place to share the depths and complexity of our hearts.
9. Authentic relationships require gut-level communication, openness, and honesty.
10. The best romantic relationships are the ones where both people are committed to honesty, communication, and openness, where issues are dealt with lovingly and quickly.
11. There is no higher expression of courage and love than the love found in our romantic relationships. Romantic love goes beyond want; it fulfills a deep human need.
12. We are at our absolute human best when we are giving and receiving love.

**WORTHY Soul Reflection Questions:**

1. In what ways have you allowed fear to quiet you from expressing your real feelings in relationships? How will you change this?

2. How have your past unhealed wounds hindered your transparency and freedom in your current relationships? What will you do to change this?

3. What is your biggest fear or limiting belief about romantic love? What are you committed to doing to heal this?

4. In what ways has regret, guilt, and past shame hindered you from engaging and being transparent in your romantic relationships? What are you committed to doing to change this?

5. How have your feelings of unworthiness affected your relationships? How will you transform this?

**WORTHY Affirmation:**

"I am lovable and worthy of love. I attract healthy love into my life."

# Key Four: Compassion

### COMPASSION AND SELF-CARE

"But this revolutionary act of treating ourselves tenderly can begin to undo the aversive messages of a lifetime."
– Tara Brach

A decade ago, after rising from the ashes of a life-altering bout with depression, I made a firm decision; I made soul-care a priority. Soul-care is a reflection of self-love. I decided to be intentional about slowing down, creating a life prioritized by the proper care of my body, mind, and emotional well-being. I would make more time for rest, fun, exercise, relationship connections, spiritual growth and simply **being.**

Since making that decision, a daily morning soul-care ritual has been a crucial component of my ongoing well-being. I invest the first hour of every morning for my personal prosperity and honor. Only when we spend time in quiet reflection time are we renewed to serve others.

Why is it that we expect others to give us the respect and attention we have refused to provide ourselves? Carve out a daily soul-care practice. Whether it is ten minutes or two hours a day, you deserve it. Self-compassion is the power to be nurturing, gracious, loving, and patient with ourselves. You are worthy of nothing less.

Self-compassion recognizes that if we are running on empty, our influence, impact, and relevance will be minimal. Self-compassion is the ability to be kind to ourselves.

## IS SELF-COMPASSION SELFISH?

> "The art of being yourself at your best is the art of unfolding yourself into the personality you want to be. Learn to love yourself, be gentle with yourself; to forgive yourself, for only as we have the right attitude toward ourselves, will we have the right attitude toward others."
> – Wilfred Peterson

Throughout our lives, we have been conditioned to believe that prioritizing our wants and needs is unwarranted, unjust, and downright selfish. Often we think that too much focus on self will turn us into narcissistic monsters – incapable of loving and caring for others. So, we go about our lives, neglecting our own needs simply because it's what we are accustomed to doing. Self-nurturing does not make you selfish; it makes you wise. Self-care is not a luxury; it is an act of survival. Taking care of yourself enhances your effectiveness, wisdom, vision, and expands your capacity to give.

Self-compassion follows the golden rule, "Love others as you love yourself." It allows you to practice what you preach. It permits you to show yourself the same loving-kindness that you would show someone else, to treat yourself with the same compassion as you would a friend.

You may notice that people who are harsh and cruel to others lack self-compassion. They treat others with the same harsh judgment and cruelty to which they subject their hearts. It starts at home. We cannot give what we do not own. We cannot offer what we do not possess. To show compassion to others, we must first show understanding, forgiveness, and kindness to ourselves.

Free yourself from self-inflicted judgment. Perfection is not the goal -- growth is. Release yourself from the mental prison of self-condemnation. You deserve to be kind to yourself; you're all you've got.

Self-compassion gives us grace, space, and freedom. Being at ease with ourselves is a profound and priceless gift.

## DOES SELF-COMPASSION SET YOU UP TO BE A SLACKER?

> "I found in my research that the biggest reason people aren't more self-compassionate is that they are afraid they'll become self-indulgent. They believe self-criticism is what keeps them in line. Most people have gotten this wrong because our culture says being hard on yourself is the way to be."
> – Dr. Kristin Neff

I have witnessed people boast of being hard on themselves as if harshness is a spiritual virtue. Being hard on ourselves does not inspire deeper insights, sustainable change, or lasting peace; it only creates more deep-seated self-doubt. Mentally berating ourselves creates feelings of soul-destroying guilt. We become guilty. What do guilty people deserve?

Yes, you guessed it, punishment. When we live with feelings of false guilt, we invite punishment into our lives in the form of relationship pain, financial loss, and unnecessary struggle. We do not deserve that. Letting ourselves off the hook requires courage. Genuine guilt inspires purification and cleansing through beautiful repentance. Repentance means to turn away. Repentance is a cleansing fire that expresses itself through a heart humbled before God's grace. It is not an ongoing process of shame and condemnation, which is a slow death. The need to confess where we lost sight of God and ourselves is holy. It encourages new, liberated, forward movement. Condemnation is soul-killing; It keeps us stuck in self-suffering, and not accepting our liberation through God's ever-present grace and mercy.

## SELF-ACCEPTANCE IS FREEDOM

> "Because one believes in oneself, one doesn't try to convince others. Because one is content with oneself, one doesn't need others' approval. Because one accepts oneself, the whole world accepts him or her."
> – Laozi

Think about your friends or family who are harsh, judgmental, and critical. Do you feel relaxed in their presence? Do you feel at ease and at liberty to be yourself? Wholeness requires self-acceptance. Imagine being in a state of consistent and sustainable relaxation within. Mistakes are a reflection of growth, not personal inadequacy. The reason self-criticism is so harmful to our psyche is that it undermines the foundation of healthy self-worth. It is self-rejection. To flourish in freedom, we embrace all of who we are. We are daily evolving, learning, discovering, and mastering who we are.

## SELF-COMPASSION AND FEELING THE PAIN

> "You can have compassion for yourself- which is not self-pity. You simply recognize that 'this is tough, this hurts,' and bringing the same warmhearted wish for suffering to lessen or end that you would bring to any dear friend grappling with the same pain, upset, or challenges as you."
>
> – Rich Hanson

Self-compassion invites us to **feel**. It takes courage to be present with what we think. To make space for our feelings, to allow them to pass through and teach us the lessons they are here to provide. We can't outrun ourselves.

The truth that we may be tempted to ignore is always there just below the surface. When we are compassionate in our allowance of time, rest, and space to process our emotions, we create a safe sanctuary within. We can greet even the most painful emotions knowing "this too shall pass…" All feelings are merely passing through. And just as we are not offended by changes in the weather, we can make room for our souls to move, change, and expand in new seasons.

Often, it is not the pain that causes the suffering, but the resistance to it. To make room for ourselves, we need to practice the sacred art of simply feeling, being, breathing, resting, and reflecting. Make room for yourself to process pain. Make room for God. Permit yourself space and time to allow these feelings and emotions to pass as you handle them from the standpoint of grace. Just as you would offer words of support and comfort to a friend who is hurting, do the same for yourself.

When we find the courage to face our feelings with compassion and honesty, we come out ten times stronger than the person who avoided, repressed, or pretended not to feel. It is the mercy we show ourselves that empowers us to transform. Self-acceptance allows us to stop controlling and suppressing emotions and experience the depth and breadth of our humanity.

Being fully engaged in this human experience means we signed up for it all -- the good, the bad, the great and what we term the "ugly" feelings. Self-acceptance means I acknowledge my light as I do the dark parts of myself; I give all of me over to the purification of a loving God.

## COMPASSION TO LOVE YOURSELF

> "Have the courage to love yourself like you always wished someone would."
>
> -Vironika Tugaleva

Several months ago, I weighed myself and wept. I didn't cry because of the numbers on the scale, but because of what they represented. To me, allowing my weight to climb reflected me forgetting about myself. We often place ourselves in the background of life -- serving, helping, and tending to others while neglecting self-respect. We lack the actions that support self-love.

Loving yourself means becoming your own best friend. Honoring the self is to cultivate more profound respect and understanding with the person with whom you spend every waking hour of the day.

Vanity is not self-love. Arrogance, selfishness and conceit are often signs of more deep-rooted insecurities. Self-nurturing does not make one loud and boastful; it cultivates quiet confidence, a sacred inner knowing. When we are in a compassionate state of self-acceptance, we can offer the same love and grace to others.

Self-love means to acknowledge your heart and to stop apologizing for who you are. Self-love is to exercise, to eat better, to release the physical, emotional, and spiritual weights that hold you back from emerging in the fullness of life. Self-love provides your heart with inner-rest and calms outward striving. Self-love is refusing to be in a hostile relationship with the person you know and need the most, you. Even God must be invited, in, by you.

Self-love is not selfish; it is your sacred insurance against ill health, a weary heart, and an exhausted soul searching for love in all the wrong places. Scripture instructs us to love our neighbors as we love ourselves. **(Mark 12:30-31)** I'm convinced that the most damaging people on this earth are people who feel low about themselves because they will wound others through the filters of their low self-concept. The better you feel about yourself, the better you treat others. You can only give abundantly from a garden that you tend to diligently. When your inner-garden is well watered, you don't have to chase the butterflies. The beauty of your garden will inspire the butterflies to come to you.

There is a sacred radiance that shines from a person who is at ease with God and themselves. They enter the room, and their presence heals — a person who has found within a deep reverence and honor for their unique journey is a breath of fresh air!

So, yes, I wept when I got off the scale, and then I apologized to myself. I told myself I was sorry for not taking care of myself, just as I would apologize to a friend I wounded or a child I neglected. I asked myself for and gave myself compassionate forgiveness. Maybe it's time for you to turn the spotlight inward refuse to overlook the sacred care of self.

### COMPASSION TO REST

"There is virtue in work and there is virtue in rest. Use both and overlook neither."
– Alan Cohen

We are a society that glories in busyness! We are more active than ever in our world, with our thousands of apps, creature comforts, and technological advancements. We are also more stressed, overwhelmed, and disconnected than the generations before us. Many of us cannot remember the last time we gathered for a family meal. Instead, we order out, and everyone goes to his or her own spaces, faces glued to tiny screens. We become voyagers into the lives of others while neglecting our own. Rest in our culture has been diminished to laziness instead of a timeless principle of soul-care and wisdom. Taking time off is now filled with working vacations where we are still accessible to everyone who can send a text message. We are busy, but not always productive. We are online but not always in life. We are uploading and posting, yet often missing the Divine downloads God wants to whisper to our spirits in silence and stillness. We consume information but often lack revelation.

We have forgotten that it is in the slowing down that we get there faster.

Beyond the physical, rest is a position of the heart. We may have an outward appearance of leisure, swinging in a hammock or lying on a sofa; yet, inwardly our minds could be racing with a thousand fears and worrisome thoughts.

Likewise, another person may be engaged in intense labor and have a heart and mind at rest. When we take moments to quietly transition from one activity to the next, we give ourselves time and space to process. The pause is holy. When we complete a big event, achieve a goal, or complete a significant activity, we need time and space to ponder, reflect and think. When we schedule a time for ourselves to replenish, renew, and recharge, we are investing in our greatest asset. This life is about making the most of our time; yet, it is also about wholeness and enjoyment.

## COMPASSION TO TAKE A SABBATH DAY

> "Every person needs to take one day away. A day in which one consciously separates the past from the future. Jobs, family, employers, and friends can exist one day without any one of us, and if our egos permit us to confess, they could exist eternally in our absence. Each person deserves a day away in which no problems are confronted; no solutions searched for. Each of us needs to withdraw from the cares which will not withdraw from us."
> - Maya Angelou

God took one day of rest to reflect on the work of creation. Likewise, we need moments to unplug and restore ourselves -- body, mind, and soul. Even if we disconnect from the noise and distractions for a few hours of the day, we can recharge. We are the first generation to process this much information. Not only are we processing higher units of data than ever before, but we also must take in the countless opinions of others. Our thoughts are bombarded, overloaded, and often exhausted because we live in a culture where opinions are cheap and plentiful, but it is wisdom that is valuable and rare. We must allow ourselves breathing room, to pause, to reflect, to disengage.

Have you ever noticed that it is often in the shower, washing dishes, or tending to your garden that you'll receive clarity? Divine downloads? It's when we release ourselves from the busyness and overthinking that the answers, revelations, and inner-guidance arises.

Sabbath rest is wise. It is an opportunity to remove ourselves to see with deeper and greater clarity.

Our anxiety-driven ego can cause us to believe that if we step back, the world will fall apart without us. Not true. The moments we step back to recharge, enable us to be more focused and effective. Sabbath rest allows us to avoid illness, fatigue, and burnout. Sabbath rest provides us with the mental space to welcome fresh strategy and perspective. It takes compassion and worthiness to allow time for proper replenishment and rest.

When we consider something valuable, we don't permit abuse or overuse; we guard and protect it as precious. Sabbath rest is a time to reflect and reassess, to remove ourselves from circumstances to see more clearly. What are we striving, working, and hustling for if we do not allow ourselves the privilege of sacred, replenishing rest?

## COMPASSION TO PROPERLY GRIEVE LOSSES

> "Only people who are capable of loving strongly can also suffer great sorrow, but this same necessity of loving serves to counteract their grief and heals them."
> – Leo Tolstoy

Nobody gets through life pain-free. As much as we'd like to avoid it, it is inevitable. People die, get divorced, friendships change, people move, natural disasters occur, someone will lose a job or become ill. At some time or another, you will experience loss and the pain associated with it. The question is: How are you going to process it? Will you stick your head in the sand and avoid the pain at all costs? Or will you do the opposite? Sit in your grief until it becomes a soul shackle, debilitating you and your loved ones? There are no formulas with pain. Some of us move through grief more quickly, while others can remain in the healing process for many years.

When we are in pain, we need comfort and kindness the most. Love is patient. Don't rush your healing. Our inability to work through the pain creates prolonged suffering.

Pain is energy in motion (e-motion). If we make room for it, it will merely pass through us. If we resist it, our suffering will persist. Pain may arrive to remind us of the life we desire. Pain helps us usher in clarity and inspired change; it helps us prioritize our lives. To minimize the length of our ordeal, we must allow ourselves to feel it all. Pain is a passageway. Authentic joy and profound growth are waiting to greet us on the other side of the pain.

There will be a season soon where our pain doesn't sting where our tears leave no trace. Time alone does not heal all wounds; yet time, coupled with God's healing love, understanding, and the courage to graciously process and grieve does. God's grace and love meet us in low places. When our hearts feel shattered, Divine love draws nearer. When we are at the depths of our sorrow, God's love journeys even deeper. This love seeks us, pursues us and guides us. God's love patiently waits for us to receive Divine peace that *passes all understanding.*

It takes inner fortitude to move through the complete range of human emotions. However, with each stage of grief, we gain a little more respect for ourselves, a more definite belief in our resilience and a deeper, more intimate connection with God. Grief is where love and pain intersect. It reveals and heals our hearts.

When I was grieving the loss of my father, I accessed feelings and sorrow I never felt before. My grief revealed the depths of my love; it exposed my unrequited longing for a deeper connection with this amazing man who I had the privilege of calling Daddy. I do not believe we can only heal ties with the living; we can make peace through death. The connection to our loved ones never dies; love is infinite. Love is eternal.

Grieving loss comes in stages. Healing has many layers. Be compassionate with yourself. Allow the process to unfold. Surrender to this holy part of life's journey.

When we are in new and uncharted emotional territory, it takes enormous doses of self-kindness and patience to heal, to mourn, and to navigate change. Death, after all, in its essence, is a profound change. One of my favorite quotes is by best selling Japanese author Haruki Murakami, and it states: "**Pain is inevitable, suffering is optional.**" We create suffering in our inability to feel and eventually release the universal natural feeling of pain. Acknowledge the pain, but compassionately **refuse** to create self-inflicted-suffering.

## SELF-COMPASSION TO LET GO

"Life becomes easier when you learn to accept an apology you never got."
-Robert Brault

When we repress hurt, anger, or a lack of forgiveness, and keep it bottled up, we prolong our suffering. We bury it **alive**. These feelings have nowhere to go. They damage the host. Fear causes us to repress what love is calling us to release.

Sometimes, it is not the physical death or loss of someone we grieve for; it is the requirement of wisdom to bury it alive. We need to let go of false hope that someone will give us something that they are utterly incapable of giving. Pain heightens when our expectations exceed a person's capacity. As a healing tool, I have found it helpful to have a private burial service. I fully mourn what I desired from another human being but never received.

I have completed this self-liberating grief and burial process with members of my own family. I teach my private clients the power of letter writing for release. You get in a quiet space of reflection, and you write down exactly what you wanted from the other person, or felt like you deserved. It might be more love, respect, time, or acknowledgment. Then, you mourn, acknowledge you will not receive it, and you allow yourself to grieve the loss of it. Many of my clients engage in the purification of burning the letter to signify completion and rebirth. For many, authentic peace follows the supernatural acceptance that this writing exercise offers. The message is not for them; it is for you. It is an act of reverent self-honor and release.

We may be called to grieve our disappointed expectations of the living so that we can truly rest in peace. Wisdom teaches acceptance. The only direct control we have in life is over our attitudes and actions. We have no control over another human being. Worthiness allows us to let people go from our binding expectations.

## SELF-COMPASSION TO END REGRET

"The wins and losses will take care of themselves; the goal is to improve daily."
-Rick Fox

I had a horrible car accident when I was younger. I wrecked my mother's brand-new car, fresh off the lot. The pain I suffered emotionally was intensified by the damage done to her vehicle, coupled with the fact that my passenger, my friend, sued me. I felt confused and betrayed. I was in my early twenties, and this was my first bout with anxiety. I became paranoid and fearful when driving. A driver rear-ended me, so whenever a person would get too close to the rear of my car, I felt the uncomfortable anxiety creeping back upon me. I liken my experience to the genuine post-traumatic stress we can encounter. Our triggers serve to instruct us that there are still familiar, painful memories that require cleansing and healing release.

In seasons of life recovery and spiritual restoration, we must intentionally and compassionately live with the intention to heal past trauma. We can also accept the truth that no matter the past wins or losses, our intention to grow and evolve daily is the key to a happier and more influential life.

Life recovery and soul rehabilitation are sacred journeys. We are worthy of disarming past trauma and triggers to live with freedom in the now.

Much like a person recovering from a stroke or physical illness, we are regaining our mental and emotional strength, health, and power.

During our time of focused recovery, we may feel inspired to distance ourselves from all external triggers until we are stronger. Keeping our emotional, physical, and spiritual space protected and sacred during seasons of intentional healing is not selfish; it is wise. We are restoring our lives.

When we are free from old tapes and false regrets, we heal and flourish. If we are devoted to growth in life, we must reflect on past mistakes to evolve in personal wisdom and make better decisions. Regret, however, chains us to the past in a destructive and self-defeating way. Only by releasing old grief can we receive new wisdom.

## COMPASSION TO SAVE YOURSELF

> You are your own refuge
>
> There is no other
>
> You cannot save another
>
> You can only save yourself.
>
> – Guillaume Musso

Self-compassion empowers us to keep rising and choosing ourselves. God is our true refuge; Jesus is our savior; the Holy Spirit is our guide. We are the temple that houses the Divine. We must be a safe place for ourselves. It takes self-compassion to accept God's abundant provision over our limited understanding. It takes self-compassion to allow yourself to rest in God. We are invited in scripture to lay down the burden in exchange for the anointing of ease. In scripture, Jesus lovingly invites those who are *weary to receive the gift of heart-centered-rest.* This world's trappings will wear us down and exhaust us because unworthiness is never satisfied.

There will always be a voice reminding you of what you didn't do or what you could or should have done. Low-self-esteem keeps us distracted, over-giving, and chasing the wind.

Humility knows when *enough is enough*. The ego can be a relentless task-master. Humility knows when to rest. The compassion to surrender the entire function of my thought life to a loving and gracious God is an act of conscious humility. Gradually, day-by-day, as we grow, reclaim, and recover our lives, we begin to recognize ourselves again. We return home to the promise contained within our replenished soul. We know how to access through intimacy with God a **peace that passes all understanding.**

After my season of Soul Sabbatical, a time of deep healing and personal restoration, the lights of my soul came back on. Overcoming a paralyzing bout with depression taught me the supreme value of cultivating, renewing and nurturing my mind. Daily.

Recovery after a significant personal loss or trauma requires us to depend on God's truth rather than relying solely on *self-talk* as trauma can emotionally blind us. Our logical mind only knows what it already knows. Our intuitive heart, prompted by the Holy Spirit, will lead us on our creative healing journey. This leading of the Holy Spirit will be confirmed through signs, wonders, and Divine confirmations. Healing requires reverent attention, and an unwavering commitment to rise whole.

The need to suffer can become an addiction, a spiritual stronghold. We have authority over darkness not by wallowing in it, but by turning on the light within. By speaking and declaring the truth of God's word, we become and embody the light. Darkness cannot survive light. We are not powerless. We can learn to discern the difference between a lie and the truth. We can reject thoughts that come to steal, kill, and destroy our joy and peace. We can focus on words that bring life and cultivate wholeness in Christ. Lies diminish us. Love expands us. The deceptions we believe cause inner-accusation and create fear and panic; they reduce us. The truth of God's love expands us into deeper levels of freedom, kindness, and peace.

We are called to walk by faith. It is the unseen realm that influences this realm; scripture states: **our battle is not against flesh and blood, yet against, wickedness, and principalities in high places." (Ephesians 6:12)** There are high-places in our hearts — places where we bow down to worship the idols of fear, worry, and unworthiness.

When we bow down to the lie, we receive the fruits of anxiety, fear, emotional torment, broken trust in God, and a diminished view of life.

The path to spiritual maturity is learning how to separate the lie from the truth. The truth may sting, but it is the only thing that sets us free. We are called to be confident in Christ; yet, confidence and condemnation cannot co-exist.

Love sets the captive free; show yourself loving compassion. When emotional recovery is compassionate, you emerge whole as the best version of yourself — the most accurate, bravest, and most authentic part of you remains. I have come to be profoundly grateful for my wilderness seasons of depression, isolation, and **dark nights of the soul**. Those gut-wrenching valleys taught me how to release my fears and limitations and embrace the fullness of God's love, power, and purification. Those emotionally hard and profoundly lonely seasons taught me how to love myself and others in a way nothing else could. Your emotional breakdown is often the key to unlocking your spiritual breakthrough.

Wisdom uses pain for a purpose. Love creates significance from suffering. God increases our compassion through our challenges. Nothing you have experienced has been in vain. Everything is valuable when it is given over to the Master Creator; God, our Source, confirms in scripture that our hardships are tools of transformation, and they have an end date. ***Many are the afflictions of the righteous, but He will deliver us from them all. (Psalms 34:19)*** Yes, we have been through hardships, but the promise of restoration is ALL. All things will be restored. All problems will be solved. All needs will be met. All pain become the purposed seeds in your season of promised harvest.

Pain prioritizes our lives. It inspires us to let go of the old to make room for the new: new love, new life, new opportunities, and new relationships. As scripture reminds us, **"We cannot put new wine into old wineskins." (Mark 2:22)** The shedding of the old creates space for the glorious new. We all deserve to make peace with our past, show self-compassion in our present and lovingly expand the vision of our future.

## A WORTHY Belief

"Self-Compassion is required for wholeness, personal joy, sustainable peace, and life transformation."

## WORTHY Key Factor Takeaways:

1. Self-care is compassionate. Self-care is self-love. Self-compassion is the ability to be kind to ourselves.
2. Self-care, self-love, and self-compassion are not selfish; these daily practices make you wise.
3. Self-compassion follows the golden rule, "Love others as you do yourself." It allows you to practice what you preach.
4. Let go of false guilt. Being "guilty" and self-condemned is a hiding place for not showing up in our greatness.
5. The reason self-criticism is so harmful to our psyche is that it undermines the foundation of healthy self-worth. For love to flourish, grow, or evolve, it must first be rooted in self-acceptance.
6. Love is patient. You are worthy of patiently loving yourself.
7. Self-acceptance means I embrace my light as quickly as I do the dark parts of myself.
8. Forgiveness begins in your own heart– with yourself. You hold the key to unlocking your private mind-made prison.
9. When we are in pain, we need comfort and kindness the most.
10. Compassionate eating is releasing ourselves from overeating, harsh diets, fad weight loss gimmicks, and deciding to love ourselves at the beginning of the journey.
11. Your graciousness towards yourself empowers others.
12. Regret is an extremely damaging emotion; it gives us nothing to rebuild our lives.
13. Letting go is a gift we give to ourselves; you are worthy of letting yourself off the hook.

**WORTHY Soul Reflection Questions:**

1. In what ways have you allowed a lack of self-love to hinder you from taking care of yourself as a priority? How will you change this?

2. How would your life change if you showed yourself more kindness and grace as it relates to self-image, body image, and weight?

3. How have you allowed the destructive emotions of guilt and regret to rob you of joy, happiness, and new life? How will you heal this?

4. What can you begin doing NOW to show yourself more compassion and loving-kindness? How will you make this a daily/weekly self-care routine?

5. How would silencing the voice of your inner critic and replacing it with thoughts of self-love change your life for the better?

**WORTHY Affirmation:**

"I deserve my self-respect. I will treat myself with compassion, kindness, gentleness, and love. My goal is not perfection; my goal is growth."

# Key Five: Clarity

> "It's a lack of clarity that creates chaos and frustration. Those emotions are poison to any living goal."
> –Steve Maraboli

Flowing in clarity is a spiritual passion of mine. Guidance is something that I never take for granted, and it is nurtured daily through a relationship with the Holy Spirit. It is cultivated by practicing the timeless spiritual art of *waiting on God*. Even in times of not knowing or uncertainty, we are reminded in scripture, that we have the Holy Spirit who will **"lead and guide us into all truth." (John 16:13)** The Holy Spirit is the Spirit of comfort, and clarity comforts the soul. Guidance is a gift of God's grace. When we are clear about who we are and what our goals and objectives are, we move through life differently. Clarity makes life easier. Clarity is the ability to separate the fear-based thoughts from love-based wisdom. Fear perverts healthy thinking; faith makes things clear. Ultimately, clarity helps you discern the truth from what is false.

The ability to trust our spiritual intuition, The Holy Spirit instinct is rooted in our assessment of self-worth. God's voice must filter through your perception of self. If you always doubt yourself, you will doubt God's voice. Unhealed trauma diminishes trust in your thoughts. Unexamined thoughts and heart beliefs can have a devastating impact on our sense of worth and self-esteem. All of life flows through the filter of our hearts, minds, and souls. We spend more time with ourselves than anyone else does. Public success flourishes when we cultivate secret harmony. Learning to listen and trust the voice of God within requires the practice of our faith: prayer, reading, or meditation, fasting, silence, solitude. Stillness.

Cultivating a lifestyle that allows time for communion with our soul and the voice of God, increases joy.

## THE POWER OF INTUITION

"When we seek daily spiritual guidance, we are guided toward the next step forward for our art. Sometimes the step is very small. Sometimes the step is, "Wait. Not now." Sometimes the step is, "Work on something else for a while." When we are open to Divine Guidance, we will receive it. It will come to us as the hunch, the inkling, the itch. It will come to us as timely conversations with others. It will come to us in many ways--but it will come."
-Julia Cameron

Holy Spirit led Intuition is a spontaneous inner knowing that defies the limits of logic. The supernatural gifts of knowledge and wisdom offer spiritual understanding that surpasses over-thinking. As we evolve spiritually and become more conscious, we abandon the paralyzing habit of over-thinking. We learn to align ourselves with the gentle flow of the Holy Spirit's leading.

Distractions scream! The noise level of our culture is loud, yet the Holy Spirit is a gentle whisper. Insights are quiet. It takes practice to heed, hear, and discern the internal promptings of wisdom. Inner-guidance is freely given; however, not in the most obvious ways. I've asked for clarity only to receive a telephone call from a distant friend telling me that *I was on her heart*. We we ask, we receive, yet we do not control the channels of *how* or *when*.

You may feel an internal leading to read a book, watch a particular ministry video, visit a specific person or place. Our spirit is always guided by inner hunches that, when followed, confirm our best interest and highest path. The answers we seek are seeking us.

## THE GIFTS OF DIVINE GUIDANCE

> "Do not assume that divine guidance flows only when you are in need of help. Guidance continues to flow whether or not you have problems. It transcends problems, heartbreaks, and traumas, flowing through dreams and illuminations.
> Whether guidance comes during times of tranquility or trauma, however, it is up to you to have the courage to acknowledge it."
> -Caroline Myss

Listening to the leading of the Holy Spirit is our inner compass, our internal radar. It is our God-given navigation system. When we ignore or override this Gentle Voice of guidance, we pay the price later. As we learn to trust the inner-leading, our spiritual gifts increase with use. God will often confirm these soul-whispers through signs, wonders, and little coincidences that follow, or as author Squire Rushnell wondrously terms: "God-winks." These Divine confirmations reflect Divine Providence; they are guiding our souls each step of the way. Our predestined course is never left to chance. God is not playing games with our lives or rolling Divine dice with our destiny. There are strategies and guidance available for every endeavor. Wisdom, clarity, and intuitive knowledge are in infinite supply when we remain connected to Source.

A person with a compromised sense of worthiness will be tempted to doubt, over-think, and mistrust the inner-voice of wisdom. The fear of making a mistake plagues the mind of chronic overthinkers. Indecision and stalling diminish confidence in our God-given gifts.

Procrastination and hesitation wound our self-esteem. The guidance of the Holy Spirit is the knowledge that moves us into motion, action and Divine alignment.

The young squirrels in my backyard right now are preparing for a winter they have never experienced. These squirrels were just born in the spring, yet every day they follow their inner-guidance system, the one God gave all animals to ensure survival and procreation. They gather and store food for a season they have never experienced. They cannot question or doubt why they do it; they follow what their instinctual nature prompts them to do.

God declares that man reflects and embodies the Divine. Made in God's image, blessed with a capacity to evolve, expand, and co-create, we have a higher ability for intuitive insight than any other living creature.

We have an innate power to sustain life and activate vision beyond the boundaries of sight. It requires practice, faith, and belief to increase your trust in the gifts of knowledge and wisdom that the Holy Spirit gives. It takes confidence to act upon the internal signals you are receiving, and it takes humility to position your heart to receive and trust the fantastic gift of guidance.

## CLARITY AND SELF-CONFIDENCE

> "It takes courage to grow up and become who you are."
> – E. E. Cummings

Who were you before this world's fears and society's limitations attempted to rob you of the knowing within your soul? Clarity is not about adding more to your life. It is about releasing the false beliefs and old mentalities that no longer accurately reveal the person you are becoming. When we live free from limiting thoughts and ideas, clarity can flourish. Soul level clarity builds confidence. It empowers you to move forward. It allows you to shine in the authentic truth of who you are. People with low self-esteem tend to shy away from new opportunities. Open doors can be scary for those who lack a firm belief in their competency.

Healthy self-esteem is having faith in your competence. It empowers your ability to rise to the occasion and handle new situations appropriately. People with a healthy concept of self readily accept new opportunities outside of their immediate realm of comfort. They move forward and trust that clarity will flourish as they move. Clarity increases confidence. The inner, intuitive knowing that flows from clarity helps to combat analysis paralysis. Indecision is painful. Mental vacilating and fearing future shame or humiliation is soul-killing. The fear of making the wrong choice robs people of the ability to learn and grow in their gifts. We learn as we go; we are still moving forward. At least mistakes offer us feedback; they provide us with proof of where we are out of alignment and need to make a course correction. Analysis paralysis keeps us stuck and hindered by our imaginary fears.

Fear, at times, is the rational response. The danger is real. However, the majority of the mental worries that paralyze us from leaving our comfort zone are not about a real threat; these vain imaginings are an illusion. Fear is one of our most consistent enemies. Clarity helps you discern valid concerns from fear-based fantasy.

## CLARITY VS. SURRENDER

> "The more you go with the flow of life and surrender the outcome to God, and the less you seek constant clarity, the more you will find that fabulous things start to show up in your life."
> —Mandy Hale

Needing to know everything with certainty can also hinder your peace, your inner-tranquility. We are all still living, learning, and experiencing our way to more profound answers and truth.

I believe in the beauty and mystery of life. On this journey, you will find yourself vacillating between the need for clarity and the beauty of trust in God to what remains uncertain. Through surrender, we find acceptance, which allows our soul to exhale.

Learning to leave room in life for the mysteries and not-knowing deepen our strength and faith. This sacred wholeness walk is a subtle paradox of calling forth and letting go; fighting on and surrender; dark and light; pain and beauty; being clear and feeling uncertain.

Surrender is often the hardest spiritual act to initiate, yet it makes life more comfortable to live in. We can exhale. We can give up our obsessive need to control the outcome as we learn to rely on the God who determines the outcome.

## WHAT IF WE WERE WRONG IN OUR THINKING?

> "As a single footstep will not make a path on the earth, so a single thought will not make a pathway in the mind. To make a deep physical path, we walk again and again. To make a deep mental path, we must think over and over the kind of thoughts we wish to dominate our lives."
>
> – Henry David Thoreau

Our lives will change after we change our thinking. We attract what we focus on the most. We are more powerful than we think. The thoughts, beliefs, and feelings that we accept as truth keep showing up. How can we experience a newfound vision if old thoughts are running the mental show?

When we waste our energy thinking about what we lack, or don't have, we replay the familiar story of "not enough" and call the usual back into existence. Often, our future projections create fear. Dwelling on the past causes us to forfeit the power of the moment.

Each time we allow our undisciplined and untrained minds to wander about, we disconnect from inner peace. Clarity comes with taking one day at a time.

Experiencing happiness in life is a reflection of devotion to cultivating our minds and souls. The inner-life determines the healthiness of outer life.

A calm mind and a heart at rest is a glorious gift. The ability to remain peaceful within means you are flowing in a level of supreme trust. You are not disturbed continuously and moved by outer circumstances; you have an internal anchor of peace in God that passes all understanding. A serene soul is a byproduct of clarity of Source and a heart at rest.

## SURRENDER AND CLARITY

"There comes a time in life when you must make the difficult decision to let certain things go: a negative attitude that you know no longer serves you; a relationship where you are dying together, rather than growing together; an addiction that you know is destroying you and does not represent your highest good."

It takes courage to face the truth about who you are, the choices that you have been making in your life and to decide; that is just not me anymore. I can't do this anymore. I have had it.

It takes a level of self-love, of dedication and determination to live your greatest life. Life is about surrendering and releasing. Surrendering to the higher calling of your life and releasing all of the things, habits, and behaviors that no longer serve you."

– Les Brown

Surrender is the beginning of restoration and new life. It is a humble request for Divine Intervention. It invites God's help.

Like the caterpillar entering the darkness of the cocoon, we will emerge in our new, pure form after the struggle of uncertainty and darkness. The lasting wisdom and clarity that follows our difficult wilderness seasons add richness, beauty, and depth to our lives like nothing else. As the brilliant author, Richard Bach, states: *What the caterpillar calls the end of the world, the Master calls the butterfly.*

As we evolve, our conscious mind grows in its ability to co-create a life that is a more authentic reflection of our deepest held desires. We learn to live emotionally above the temporary, shifting circumstances of life. We permit ourselves to live free from our past.

We begin to understand that evolving is being and becoming conscious. The dictionary describes conscious as "to be awake; to understand." Our minds, thoughts, will, and emotions are influenced, directed, strengthened, or weakened by our current state of consciousness. What we perceive to be real is real. Our perceptions are often attached to unclean filters. Fear is a filter that distorts truth and clarity. When we are unconscious, we view life as a place to prove, defend, and protect ourselves. When we live in a chronic reactionary state, we will find ourselves in continual defense mode, drained from our creative energy. Growth requires stretching. Growth can be painful and costly, but its rewards are peaceful and priceless.

## CLARITY THROUGH CONSCIOUS FREEDOM

> "There is a voice that doesn't use words. Listen."
> -Anonymous

Joy is a few steps beyond our comfort zone. Most of us have a room in the house of our consciousness where we will not allow the natural light of love to shine in. That room is usually an area where we have experienced pain. We protect that dark room by closing our hearts to God.

The stories that we tell ourselves in this distorted state of thought are not always true. Fear and unworthiness are tormenting spirits that invite deception -- self-deception.

As we read God's Word, meditate, engage in reflective thought, pray, examine, relax, and release through repentance the patterns of thinking that harm rather than help our minds' state of health, we come up higher. We re-engage the walk of faith in God.

As we mature in spiritual growth, old thoughts and addictive emotional patterns fall away. It is always darkest before the dawn, yet seeds grow in the moonlight as well as the sunlight. On the other side of the night is the morning. On the other side of pain are a purpose and abundant joy, in the midst of both is the grace of God's guidance. The path of spiritual growth is an ongoing lifestyle; yet, we can reach a place where joy, inner peace, and calm become our everyday states of being.

## FEAR OR LOVE?

*"If you realized how powerful your thoughts are, you would never think a negative thought."*
– Peace Pilgrim

Fear puts a distorted lens over our lives and casts a blinding shadow over vision. Fear is a liar. When we listen to "voices" that are deceptive, we become ensnared by the lie. We cannot live passively in our faith. As American historian, playwright and author Howard Zinn stated, ***"You can't be neutral on a moving train."*** This world is moving, filled with trappings, addictions, distractions, and diversions to our destiny and true identity. We must put on a scripture states, "the full armor of God." **(Ephesians 6:11-18)** To protect our souls from the unceasing assault on our God-given value. When your true identity is compromised, you can be swayed or convinced that you "are" or "need" whatever culture is promoting at the moment to be worthy.

We are rising to reclaim all that was lost or stolen when we accepted the lie rather than stood for the truth. Thoughts that harm us are not passive; they are active, aggressive full-frontal attacks. Passivity in faith is a powerless position. It does not honor our values nor our destiny.

We must read and study to recondition our minds and be intentional about healing and aligning with the truth of our destiny. We spend our time chasing outward things and have no inner-peace. The Kingdom comes first, then outer life aligns. The kingdom of God is righteous, peace, and joy. The inner-work of cultivating the Kingdom, creates external abundance.

It takes strength to re-examine our thinking. There have been seasons of life where I was not mentally, emotionally, and spiritually strong enough to face certain aspects of myself. It was only when my self-worth expanded that I dared to face the role my beliefs were playing in creating my moments of downfall and destiny. We are often unconscious of the limitations we have placed around our hearts, the gilded cages in which we have locked ourselves. Life is not lacking in resources, abundance, opportunities, or possibilities. We are limited by what we think and speak and believe.

What if prosperity, and peace were a function of our minds? As spiritual awareness grows, we notice a pattern with the *soul-lies* that whisper to us; they create more fear, and increase our doubts about self. The soul-lies of false-accusation create panic. Truth ushers in *relief*.

Truth shatters and exposes deception. The truth may momentarily wound us, but it will produce lasting wisdom and peace. The truth may hurt, but it ultimately reveals and heals us. When the truth comes, there is a gentle pace of recovery, Divine assistance offered to help you process, embrace, and live it.

We can rise above the tyranny of undisciplined thinking patterns. We can denounce the thoughts that come to diminish, create panic, or confuse our minds.

## THE GREATEST ENEMY OF CLARITY AND SELF-WORTH

"Internalized shame becomes the foundation of unworthiness and personal trauma. Abandonment is always beneath shame. Not receiving the necessary psychological or physical protection equals abandonment. Shame arises from the painful message implied in abandonment. "You are not important; you are not of value." Unresolved pain of the past and pain in the present created by fear-based behaviors fuel our fear of abandonment and shame. This is the pain we need to heal."
– Claudia Black Ph.D.

Shame is a liar. As author and researcher, Brené Brown states, "Shame corrodes the very part of us that believes we are capable of change." Shame attacks the very foundation of a person's soul. Shame is a destroyer of self-worth. It destroys our ability to trust ourselves and God. When we don't trust ourselves, we lack clarity, focus, and determination. Shame undermines our very right to exist.

When a person struggles with deep-rooted feelings of shame from unresolved issues in their past, it affects their ability to handle present pain or to move forward in clarity and freedom. The inner gravitational pull of low self-worth will pull a person right back down to the level of existence with which they are most familiar. If I desire a better life, but internally struggle with believing that I am worthy, shame wins. The deep belief that there is something wrong with me will cause me to create a reality that mirrors and reaffirms this belief.

If we are harboring secret shame, it is only a matter of time before circumstances show up in life to validate our inner fears of unworthiness. Healing shame may require working with a qualified professional, a therapist, or a spiritual counselor. Being intentional about cultivating spiritual wholeness and emotional freedom is a function of healthy self-worth and self-love. Embracing clarity means first releasing unhealthy shame.

## PRACTICAL CLARITY FOR LIFE'S CHOICES AND DECISIONS

> "You must read, you must persevere, you must sit up nights, and you must inquire, and exert the utmost power of your mind. If one way does not lead to the desired meaning, take another; if obstacles arise, then still another; until, if your strength holds out, you will find that clear which at first looked dark."
> – Giovanni Boccaccio

Read. Study. Listen. Think. Reflect. Read more. Develop and deepen your spiritual and emotional intellect. Our mind's intelligence and brilliance increases and expands with use. Learn to nurture and develop your inner wisdom through daily spiritual practice and quiet devotion to God. The Holy Spirit's guidance is authentic power. Learning to hear that gentle Divine voice of direction within is a rewarding journey. When we nurture clarity through an intentional relationship with God, we can handle all of life better. Clarity feels welcome in a calm, peace-centered state of mind. When we are worried, stressed, or fatigued, our thoughts become distorted with fear-based messages, half-truths, accusations, and paranoia. When we are anxiously rushing, we may miss the truth. When we intentionally slow down in our thinking, we receive direction faster. Patience reveals the truth.

When we create what I call a daily soul care routine, we reorder our private lives and minds. Self-mastery does not mean you will avoid the pain of getting knocked down; it means you get back up more quickly.

The charge is on us to renew our minds, reorder our thinking, and capture runaway, harmful thoughts. Emotions follow your thoughts, not the other way around. If you feel anxious in your heart, you will begin thinking and meditating upon worrisome thoughts. If you fear in your heart, you will rehearse thoughts that intensify the illusion of dread and doom. We can heal our hearts through compassionate and conscious focus; we can reclaim authority over our thought life.

We are charged in scripture to think about good things; **(Philippians 4:8)** meditating on good things produces a good life. Practicing gratitude and appreciation provides inner-calm and joy. Clarity feels welcome in a calm mind. You are worthy of creating and nurturing a thought life that reflects God's strongest desire for your happiness, freedom, and peace.

## A WORTHY Belief

"Clarity is required for inner peace. Clarity helps us cultivate a sound, calm mind. Clarity deepens soul level discernment and direction."

**WORTHY Key Factor Takeaways:**

1. Clarity is the ability to separate the fear-based thoughts from the love-based ones.
2. Not trusting and developing our thinking is dangerous. When we forfeit our right to think for ourselves, we are more easily led astray by another person's agenda.
3. Mental health is everything! All of life flows through the filter of our minds.
4. Public success flourishes when we uphold private order.
5. We deepen our emotional intelligence through continual learning, reading, thinking, meditation, and journal writing.
6. We attract what we focus on the most. We are more powerful than we think. The thoughts, beliefs, and feelings that we accept as truth keep showing up.
7. A calm mind is a glorious gift. A serene soul is a byproduct of soul level clarity of thought.
8. Embracing clarity and self-worth means first releasing shame. If we are harboring secret guilt or shame, it is only a matter of time before circumstances show up in life to validate our inner fears of unworthiness.
9. Clarity thrives in a calm, peace-centered state of mind.
10. There is no more significant investment than the time you devote to your personal growth and healing.

## WORTHY Soul Reflection Questions:

1. How have indecision and the fear of making a mistake (being exposed or shamed) caused you to become passive and paralyzed in life?

2. What action steps will you take to make soul care and daily spiritual devotional time a priority?

3. How will a daily spiritual practice help you cultivate inner peace? How will you release the things that don't bring you inner peace?

4. In what ways has overriding your gut instincts and inner guidance impacted your self-esteem and self-confidence?

5. What are the limiting beliefs you need to release so that your soul can thrive?

**WORTHY Affirmation:**

"Each day, I cultivate and nurture clear thinking. I walk in wisdom and clarity in my decision-making. I embrace peace, self-care, and self-love daily. I am worthy of nothing less."

# Key Six: Character

**BEING VS. DOING**

"The final forming of a person's character lies in their own hands."
— Anne Frank

When we are striving to be accepted by God, we forget that we already are. When we embrace our worthiness, we stop fearfully living *for* God's approval and start living with ease and flow *from* God's approval.

We are already *enough* not because of what we do, but because of who we are. Our gifts and achievements don't define us; we define them.

Striving and people-pleasing aimed at trying to prove our worth are exhausting: *we are worthy of love.*

I am not suggesting that great joy and profound fulfillment aren't achieved by diligently pursuing your dreams, destiny, or personal calling. I believe our most significant source of joy and fulfillment in life comes from engaging in meaningful, purpose-driven work that honors the design of our soul.

Seasons change. The roles and assignments of your calling will change. When the storms of change, loss, and transition come, we need a deeper hold on our identity that will sustain us through the outer blows of life. It helps during times of transition to maintain an inner anchoring of identity-based on our *being* not merely our *doing*.

## THE POWER OF HUMILITY

"If you are humble, nothing will touch you, neither praise nor disgrace, because you know what you are."
– Mother Teresa

The root word humility comes from the Latin word humilitas, which may be translated as grounded or "from the earth." Humility is a safe foundation from which to build self-worth. Humility is our dependence on God. Living apart from God in willful self-dependence weakens us because we are limited. We are not wise, expansive, or powerful enough to be our own Source. This world teaches people to "live their truth!" Worthiness inspires my choice to live in alignment with God's highest truth. God's dreams are more significant and bold than mine; God's vision surpasses my sight. God has limitless realms of wisdom and knowledge I can't even begin to fathom. Dependence on God is the beginning of wholeness and self-esteem, as we view ourselves through the clarity and completion of our Creator's eyes.

People who lack healthy self-worth are often tempted to overcompensate. They may be tempted to perform outwardly to settle the plaguing soul questions within. *Am I adequate? Am I lovable? Am I worthy?*

Unworthiness strives to perform, please and prove, these actions are layers of self-protection. When we are at peace within, it reflects in our outward demeanor. We show up in genuine power and a calm *inner knowing*. Humility depends on an ability higher than itself. I love the quote that states: **"Confidence gives you the courage to do what you came to this earth to do; humility gives you the capacity to be the person you came here to be."**

Confidence grants us the power to accomplish, while humility provides us with the grace to become.

## NURTURING PEACE IN YOUR PRIVATE WORLD

"Peace I leave with you; my peace I give you. I do not give to you as the world gives. Do not let your hearts be troubled and do not be afraid."

– Jesus

Peace is an inner-working of the soul that chooses to accept the completed work on the cross. Every gift comes with a need to be opened and received. Many of us confess our faith but do not execute it, and live the fullness of what it offers. Peace is priceless. Peace is what everyone in the world is seeking. Peace is worth more than silver and gold. Without peace, our material gain means nothing. Embracing God's peace in our private time creates joy and fulfillment in our most public hours. Private spiritual practice always brings open, public reward. Outward success is determined by what we do publicly. Clarity, wholeness, and peace are cultivated by who we are becoming privately.

Some of us are addicted to the outer life. We rush from one activity to the next, distracted from the real matters of the heart. Until we find the courage to slow down and look within, we will continue to miss incredible opportunities for more profound growth and joy. As our self-worth expands, so will our desire to care for ourselves in deeper and more profound ways. Love yourself by taking time each morning to refresh and recharge your mind, body, and spirit.

As Mother Teresa so beautifully stated: *Silence, solitude, and stillness are friends of God.*

These timeless spiritual disciplines invite Divine direction, soul replenishment and direct revelation. Conformed to a fearfully anxious culture, we've lost the powerfully spiritual art of "Waiting on God." Resisting this level of soul care in our lives will only create more of a need for it. One moment of Divine clarity can impact your entire day or month. One moment of inspiration can give you the answer to something that has plagued you for years, decades even. One intuitive insight can change the entire course of your life. Investing time in a daily soul care ritual and stillness with God provides consistent returns of wisdom, clarity, and sustainable peace. What better gift can you give to those you love than your own wholeness? All your relationships and business endeavors will thrive as you keep evolving within.

## THE PROFOUND NEED FOR MIND RENEWAL

"Do not conform to the pattern of this world, but be transformed by the renewing of your mind."
– Romans 12:2

We view life through the filter of our beliefs. Our beliefs shape our character. Fear-based thoughts distort the screen through which we view life. The ability to see clearly is in direct relationship with our filter. If we forfeit the personal responsibility to renew our minds and take ownership of our thinking, we become victims of people, places, and circumstances. Renewing our minds daily is a conscious decision. Our minds can become cluttered and polluted, so they need daily purification and cleaning.

We all meditate daily. We either meditate on good thoughts that add value to our lives, or we meditate on painful, worrisome thoughts that diminish our lives. Most of us have one or two predominant toxic thoughts. These negative thoughts diminish the joy and personal freedom. Just as quickly as we can imagine all that can go wrong, we can ask: "What if it goes right?" We can break our addictive devotion to the thoughts and feelings that reintroduce us to feelings of condemnation and shame.

What we believe we become. What we focus on expands. We must be devoted to spending time each day renewing our thinking. Our faith requires our participation.

Daily spiritual practice is key to healing and releasing the thoughts that destroy rather than build confidence. Our thinking habits can be changed, transformed, and re-routed to thinking that produces and co-creates the destiny we desire. Choosing new thoughts means adopting a new life.

Years of habitual, unchecked, and unexamined thinking causes us to believe that we must bow down to limiting thoughts. When we agree with God's view of us, we become limitless.

## SURRENDER IS THE BIRTHING PLACE OF VICTORY

> "The reason why many are still troubled, still seeking, still making little forward progress is because they haven't yet come to the end of themselves. We're still trying to give orders, and interfering with God's work within us."
> – A.W. Tozer

People fear the word surrender. It evokes feelings of learned helplessness, powerlessness, and profound vulnerability. For the heart that struggles with trust, surrender seems to be an invitation to more pain. Your worldview determines your view of the word surrender. If you believe the world is harsh, dangerous, and hard, you will not accept the spiritual practice of surrender.

Our ability to surrender means we knowingly invite Divine help and intervention. Surrender opens us up to greater possibilities while relieving us of the burden of false control.

Resistance is often rooted in fear. Surrender is freedom.

I'm inspired by the Asian spiritual philosophy that states: *"Be like water making its way through cracks. Do not be assertive, but adjust to the object, and you shall find a way around or through it. If nothing within you stays rigid, outward things will disclose themselves. Be like water."*

Water is the softest and yet most potent substance. Water is formless, flowing, and yielding. It powerfully carves out the landscapes of endless miles of dangerous, rigid rocks. The surrendered person is flexible and flows like water in genuine strength.

Forcing, controlling, and attempting to manage every aspect of life leaves no room for the subtle, beautiful mysteries of God. When we release and relax, we can allow and receive.

Authentic peace follows letting go of false control. Surrender is when we stop toiling, protecting and striving, and we begin receiving, accepting, and arriving. Nothing is more beautiful than to experience the inner rest that follows surrender. It is a glorious gift to live with a calm mind and a soul at ease.

## THE CALL TO PRIVATE ORDER

> "At the end of your life, you will never regret not having passed one more test, not winning one more verdict or not closing one more deal. You will regret time not spent with a husband, a friend, a child, or a parent".
>
> – Barbara Bush

At one point in my life, my drive and ambition had become a quest to measure, achieve, strive, and prove my worth.

My three young sons were often last on the priority list of emails, business emergencies, and ministry expansion. They would often get what was left over after other people, strangers even, received my best. I was looking for something that I already possessed — waiting on something I already had: *unconditional love*.

Driven by ego, it is easy to neglect the relationships, self-nurturing, spiritual devotion and simple truths that create authentic joy. I knew that I could no longer give to others what I failed to give myself and the members of my own family. Healing starts at home.

When I walked away from a business I ran for over ten years, I felt the sting of death. When you are driven, you have a sense of ownership over your dream -- it *is* you. It becomes your whole identity. So, when you choose to step away, you can feel lost, disconnected from truth, and unable to find a sense of wholeness or worthiness without it. When you accept your calling, you are simply a carrier, a vessel of the gift. You operate in the freedom of stewardship. The calling reveals God's glory through you.

What I perceived as a public failure in the closing of my business was the stepping-stone to my inevitable victory. In allowing God to divinely and strategically expose the false mental foundation that ego built and create structural integrity within, I found sustainable peace. I no longer wanted to be driven; I wanted to be called. In that profound season of life change, I witnessed first-hand that when we come to the end of ourselves, God's power begins.

## GUILT AND GRACE

> "Let us then approach God's throne of grace with confidence, so that we may receive mercy and find grace to help us in our time of need."
> – Hebrews 4:16

When we allow our view of God to become distorted by past mistakes, we step into a downward spiral of rejection. Rejection hurts, especially when it is self-inflicted. Unworthiness will make us afraid to hope, to dream; it will bring us into a familiar cycle of expecting disappointment. We are not our experiences; we are alchemists, working in co-creative collaboration with our Source. When we agree with God's view of us, we release our need to suffer; we open our hearts to the power of grace and mercy. We go *through the valley of the shadow of death* and awaken on the other side with greater resilience, wisdom, and character. This high calling is the cost of our former life. It is a surrender of the small, unworthy self. To exchange our shame for God's significance, to exchange our guilt for God's grace, to find ourselves, we must first lose ourselves. The high calling comes at a cost. It will cost you your unworthiness, your devotion to self-doubt. It will cost you your approval addiction and your need to hold yourself hostage to old regrets and dead stories. The High calling is an exchange for the life we've constructed from our limited sight and a gift given of the life we receive through Divine vision. You are worthy of God's restoration and grace; this is your new beginning.

You are worthy of experiencing the fullness and beauty of all God destined. To take the path of worthiness is to agree with God's opinion of you, rather than live in constant resistance. It is to offer yourself and your loved ones, a living example of the legacy of love, joy and peace.

## **CHARACTER AND THE POWER TO FORGET**

"I can forgive, but I cannot forget, is only another way of saying, I will not forgive. Forgiveness ought to be like a canceled note - torn in two, and burned up so that it never can be shown against one.
– Henry Ward Beecher

When I was at the lowest point of my depression several years ago, I began to see my thought patterns. I was stewing, sitting in my pain, just allowing old memories to live on and fester. My pain was not coming from any current challenges, but remembering the past deepened my suffering. Emotionally healthy people forget and move on.

One day, as I was attending one of my private "pity parties," I heard the gentle voice of Divine wisdom say: "Sanity is nurtured by forgetting."

Wow. Lights on! I was making myself crazy because I refused to *forget* the pain. I refused to forget the mistakes. I allowed my ego and unworthiness to hold me hostage to a debt I no longer owed. Repentance and grace paid it in full.

The moment I decided to start forgiving and forgetting, my mind began to heal, and my peace returned. True happiness and freedom are nurtured not only in forgiveness but also in forgetting. Forgetting past offenses is a critical factor in creating heart rest.

A mind cluttered with past thoughts, old conversations, and unhealed wounds can only serve to drag us down and compromise our ability to live freely. Suffering can become an addiction. Choosing to release the old story is a byproduct of self-love and reverence for God's grace and forgiveness in our lives. It takes self-worth to release past pain. Our mistakes become our miracles. Our regrets become the birthing ground of our restoration. Grace waters the seeds of our harvest. God loves a good "reversal of the odds" story. Nothing is wasted; our pain becomes the raw building material of the promise. We strengthen in courage and power when we consciously decide to leave the story behind and move forward in the direction of our destiny.

## CHARACTER AND FORGIVENESS

"It is very important for every human being to forgive herself or himself because if you live, you will make mistakes - it is inevitable. But once you do and you see the mistake, then you forgive yourself and say, 'Well, if I'd known better I'd have done better,' that's all. So, you say to people whom you think you may have injured, 'I'm sorry,' and then you say to yourself, 'I'm sorry.' If we all hold on to the mistake, we can't see our own glory in the mirror because we have the mistake between our faces and the mirror; we can't see what we're capable of being. You can ask forgiveness of others, in the end, the real forgiveness is in one's own self."

– Maya Angelou

Self-forgiveness is a higher spiritual practice. It is the intentional preservation of inner peace. When you love someone, you don't want to see them suffer needlessly. Refusing to offer ourselves forgiveness is self-abandonment. I once heard it stated: *"Forgiveness is a radical act of self-love."* Wallowing around in old regrets is self-cruelty. God is a loving God. God is a forgiving God. The cliché, "confession is good for the soul" is based on truth. Guilt will eat a person alive. When we confess our shortcomings, we begin to heal truly.

Forgiving ourselves gives us the power of new energy in motion; it is the ability to learn, adjust, and course-correct. When we refuse to let ourselves off the hook for past behaviors, we don't benefit from the lessons learned. When we forgive ourselves, we transmute the energy of past mistakes into the currency of powerful wisdom. Nobody is exempt from the pain and struggle of being human. As long as we live on this earth, we will struggle. God does not demand human perfection, God rewards spiritual faith. We all have moments of anxiety, guilt, regret, doubt, and paralyzing fear, but the real sign of self-mastery is the length of time we spend with these emotions.

As evolving beings, our recovery time occurs more quickly. We show ourselves grace. We correct our mistakes. We compassionately refuse to wallow in dead-stories and dead places. We pick ourselves up and press on. We forgive. As we learn to quickly forgive and forget offenses as a spiritual commitment and way of life, we can accelerate our healing and resilience to bounce back. If an emotional blow used to knock you down for three years, you might now recover in three weeks. As you mature, what used to hold you emotionally hostage for three days can now be released in three hours. Wholeness offers a quicker recovery time. Forgiving others and ourselves is a profound act of self-love and a reflection of spiritual maturity.

## CREATING THE HABIT OF FORGIVENESS

"Forgiving what we cannot forgive creates a new way to remember. We change the memory of our past into a hope for our future."
- Lewis Smedes

The journey of **Worthy** is not complete until we are living in freedom. An unforgiving nature is soul slavery. Anger holds the spirit in prison. Until we release the person who we are holding hostage to the past offense, we will be emotionally caged and spiritually shackled. We deserve better. We deserve the beauty of personal liberty. We deserve a better future, one aligned with God's grace, goodness, and mercy.

Forgiveness is easier when there has been a focus on inner healing first. The intention to forgive is what starts the healing process. Rushed, obligatory forgiveness given out of guilt can feel cheap and shallow. The decision to forgive means you are choosing to recover your truth and life. You are deciding nothing, and no one is worth impeding your relationship with yourself. Forgiveness does not forsake wisdom. Many times in life, depending upon the severity of the wound or the maturity of our spiritual walk, forgiveness may take time and come in layers. The intention to forgive, to be free from an "offended state" of being is vital. We cannot expect God to violate spiritual law. Our offenses are forgiven *as we forgive* others. There isn't anything or anyone on this earth who is worthy of hindering our relationship with our Creator or our future destiny.

Forgiveness does not always mean reconciliation; it means we release the other person and ourselves graciously back into God's care and understanding. Forgiveness and love are tempered by wisdom. Some relationships are unsafe, destructive, or not conducive to our emotional growth or spiritual wellbeing. While love always calls us to forgive, wisdom may request us to maintain healthy boundaries.

The higher we rise in spiritual growth, the more we understand our power to re-frame the energy of another person's shortcomings through compassion and understanding. As we release them, we free ourselves. As we extend mercy to others, it flows through and purifies our hearts. The gift of grace we give is the gift of grace we receive.

Life is a boomerang; the kindness we show is the kindness we reap. Any ill feelings we hold toward another invites pain into our lives. As scripture states in the law of biblical attraction: **we reap what we sow. (Galatians 6:7)** We cannot hurt another person without hurting ourselves. We cannot bless another human being without blessing ourselves. We are all connected, children of God. There is no lasting peace or totality of freedom without forgiveness.

## CHARACTER AND THE COURAGE TO COMMIT

"Unless commitment is made, there are only promises and hopes; but no plans."
– Peter F. Drucker

We desire love. We want to create success. We want to cultivate happiness. There is a vast difference between wanting something and being committed to it. The definition of the word "commit" is to "devote oneself unreservedly." Commitment lays the foundation for solution-based action. There is a difference between *desiring* something and *deciding* to manifest it. Decisions inspire forward movement. Commitment creates focus. The universe responds favorably to both. Being solution-oriented is the only healthy, sustainable way to realize change in our lives.

To commit is to choose. Being committed to fulfilling our desires requires courage, clarity, and self-compassion. We are entering a world where we have decided to rise above self-imposed limits and hindering false beliefs. Committed people live with boldness, confidence, and soul-level-prosperity.

Commitment is the key that turns inspiration into new choices, potential into power, and beliefs into bold action. Consistency is the key to engagement. Loyalty is a universally admired trait; commitment is being loyal to the promises we make to ourselves.

Have you ever met a person and marveled at their potential and yet, year after year, never witnessed them rise to the occasion of their greatness? Commitment is the key ingredient that turns potential in actual power. People want change, but only those committed to change will create it. Commitment inspires discipline; discipline encourages us to make daily demonstrations of our faith. You are worthy to walk in a life rooted in faith, action, and commitment.

Growth is a daily goal. Change takes time. Healing takes time. Deepening your voice of inner-discernment, intuition, and spiritual gifts take time. Success takes time. Faith without patience is amplified frustration. It is not enough to want it if we are not committed to preparing for it, being prepared for it, and strengthening our endurance in the process of waiting and creating.

Each day, we can choose to live with a deeper level of character, one based on our strongest desires and intentions. We can choose to align with God's highest purpose and stop resisting our own good. There is a voice within you calling out, whispering for better. There is a voice that is reawakening you to the power, genius, and vision that you are destined to fulfill. Listen carefully. Even now, your heart is calling for more. The time is now; the person is **you.**

## A WORTHY Belief

"Character is the ability to bring order and authenticity to our private world. With a strong character, we have the foundation to build sustainable success and personal joy."

## WORTHY Key Factor Takeaways:

1. When identity is based on **outward** titles, material possessions, academic achievements, or even relationship status, we place ourselves in a very fragile state.
2. Authenticity is showing up in the truth of who you are called to be without compromise.
3. A strong character is developed by being consistent with your commitments.
4. Humility is peace. It has nothing left to prove; it merely remains open to give and receive love.
5. When self-worth is high, the need to prove ourselves is low.
6. It will take new thoughts, new ideas, new habits, and a new understanding to get us to a new season.
7. The longer we let old wounds and hurts fester, the harder it becomes to discern the truth of the original emotion.
8. A mind cluttered with past thoughts, old conversations, and unhealed wounds can only serve to drag us down and compromise our ability to live free.
9. Self-forgiveness is a daily practice of the humble and the mentally sane.
10. There is a difference between wanting something and being committed to it.
11. Commitment is the key that turns inspiration into new choices, potential into power, and beliefs into bold action. Commitment is the key to destiny.

## WORTHY Soul Reflection Questions:

1. In what ways have you diminished or swallowed your authentic voice to go along with the status quo?

2. What do you need to forgive and show yourself grace for?

3. In what ways have you merely wished for or wanted change, but have not been wholeheartedly committed to change? How will you change that?

4. In what ways do you need to bring order to your private world?

5. Who do you need to forgive and set free?

**WORTHY Affirmation:**

"I live a life that honors my deepest held values, authentic truth, and beliefs. I am growing in wisdom and understanding daily."

# Key Seven: Called

*"There is no greater gift you can give or receive than to honor your calling. It's why you were born. And how you become most truly alive."*
– Oprah Winfrey

God created you for a specific purpose. Your life is not an accident. Your life is a byproduct of thoughtful design. Answering your calling is your most magnificent journey, the one that leads you back home to the truth of who you are.

Giving God your surrendered *yes* to purpose is a tremendous act of courage. Answering your calling is a walk of bravery. It takes worth to honor your calling. It takes a quiet knowing within to understand that you were born for something unique, something more.

When Henry David Thoreau stated: "Most men lead lives of quiet desperation," he was not far off.

When we know we are worthy; we allow ourselves to create an experience that reflects our deepest inspired desires. We believe that life will be guided, directed, and provided for by a limitless Source of goodness. Inner guidance for walking in your calling is always available at any given moment. It may not come in the form of a burning bush or a neon sign, but there is consistent direction available for those who dare step into their purpose.

When we allow the resistant, fear-based mindset to take the driver's seat, our mind imagines the 99 reasons why our dream won't work. Our justifications, excuses, and fear-centered reasoning distort new possibilities and make us falsely believe that our goals are destined to fail before we even begin.

Scores of us talk ourselves out of a new idea by over-thinking into the future. Future imagined worries crowd out the gentle voice of Divine direction, a Voice whispering even now.

## THE CALL CREATES SELF-RESPECT

> "If you ask me what I came to do in this world, I, an artist, will answer you: I am here to live out loud."
> – Émile Zola

I'll never forget listening to an interview with Pulitzer Prize-winning author, Alice Walker. Her statement was so profound that it has stuck with me to this very day. She conveyed that true satisfaction did not come from the public accolades and awards that she had received for writing her books. Her most profound gift was one that she gave to herself -- the gift of *self-respect* that came each time she completed her work. Until we do the work of our soul, we will struggle with self-doubt, distractions, addictions, unhappiness, and dissatisfaction. Joy in life increases as we align with our purpose, calling, and assignment.

Wavering, stalling, procrastinating, and over-thinking are painful and paralyzing habits. Rising to the occasion of your destiny is a deliberate, daily choice. When we complete the book, the workshop, the event, the poem, the painting or step out and launch our vision, we rise in self-confidence, competence, and belief. Keeping our promises to ourselves is a profound gift; completing our work is a reflection of healthy self-love. We honor the unique imprint of our Creator's investment in us. We trust the sacred role that is ours alone in this lifetime to play.

## RESISTANCE, THE SILENT ASSASSIN OF THE CALLED

> "Most of us have two lives. The life we live and the unlived life within us. Between the two stands Resistance. Late at night, have you experienced a vision of the person you might become, the work you could accomplish, the realized being you were meant to be? Are you a writer who doesn't write, a painter who doesn't paint, an entrepreneur who never starts a venture? Then you know what Resistance is."
> – Steven Pressfield

Resistance works against us when we attempt to step into the greatness of our calling; whether it's writing a screenplay or launching a product, we encounter this unseen, invisible force. According to *The War of Art* author, Steven Pressfield, the power of resistance attempts to do one thing: "stop us from doing our work." It keeps us from achieving the unique work of our soul; the more profound the work, the stronger the fear and resistance oppose us. Feelings of inadequacy, self-doubt, and fear of public exposure or humiliation contaminate the gentle soul whisper of purpose. The question becomes this: Are we willing to let the lower things die so that, the higher may live? Are we willing to put off the short-term, temporary gratification that avoidance brings to dig deep and discipline ourselves for the greater reward in the long run?

When we get to a place where the act of avoiding, resisting, and suppressing our brilliance is excruciating, we will change; we will show up in authentic truth. Refusing to accept anything less than the purpose for which God created us, is the best form of truth and sacred rebellion.

We must honor our calling; it is our soul's most magnificent expression. The higher the attack fear wages, the more profound the gift of the soul. Resistance is a force of fear that ravages many.

Resistance will deceive us into justifying, reasoning, and excusing ourselves out of the very lives we desire and are destined to live. When we release our need to self-sabotage, we rise. Walking in our calling is not about abolishing fear. Fear will always be present.

Living our calling is about moving through the fear to honor the investment of God's love and purpose for our lives.

Your life's calling is the answer to someone's prayer. It is your unique contribution to this world. Now more than ever, we need people who are courageously brave enough to show up unapologetically in their truth. Miracles flourish when we stop resisting the truth and say **yes** to the voice within our hearts.

## STOP AVOIDING AND CHOOSE SURRENDER

> "The world won't step into its greatness until we step into ours."
> – Marianne Williamson

Surrender is allowing yourself to take the same journey of the caterpillar. In the wild, caterpillars do two things: eat and survive against predators. When you surrender to your calling, you transcend the fear-based survival world of the caterpillar. When the caterpillar enters the cocoon and begins the chrysalis process, it is dark, uncomfortable, and lonely. When we surrender to our calling, we enter the same metamorphosis. We may feel powerless, hidden, and isolated as we willingly state to God, **"Not my will, but Your will be done."**

As we emerge from our transformation, we soar. What appeared to be a threat to the caterpillar looks insignificant to the butterfly.

When we feel the most pain in surrender, it is the time of our deepest, inner transformation. It is in surrendering to the process of the calling that we access greater power and influence. We emerge whole, as beautiful butterflies, whose beauty and flight inspire. When we stop resisting ourselves, we rise above; we were created to live a life of prosperity, significance, profound love, and purpose.

## HIDING BEHIND FEAR AND CONFUSION

> "The more of me I be, The clearer I can see."
> – Rachel Archelaus

When working with my private clients, I often ask them the profound question one of my mentors once asked me: "What are you pretending not to know?" We pretend not to know what God has whispered to our hearts. We pretend not to understand why we desire what we desire. We pretend not to see a relationship is over or that we have outgrown our current environment. Life is fluid and flexible; it is always changing. It's not our job to figure it all out before we begin. Truth and miracles unfold in motion! We discover Divine strategy and guidance as we move forward. Our job is to stop hiding from ourselves, avoiding destiny, wasting precious time, and shrinking away in fear.

When I launched my relationship blog several years ago, I did so with trembling and tears. My original blog topics centered on some weighty and pressing issues that hit close to home -- my home. I explored themes of inner healing and exposed some of my most profound flaws. I feared the opinions of others. I feared their judgment, being vulnerable and exposed. Shaking and weeping, I will never forget clicking "Publish" in my WordPress dashboard. I knew I had reached the point of no return.

I reached the point where the pain of remaining behind the shadows was more profound than accessing the courage to awaken boldly in the truth of my destiny. I was no longer able to reject my own heart or deny the call of God. Most times, we allow fear to get us stuck on the question of how? Walking by faith means letting God handle how, trusting that all things are aligning for our highest good as we step forward in vision.

The profound act of committing to your vision will activate all the resources you need. *Purpose provides.* When you choose to rise despite the inner voices of fear and doubt, self-respect grows. Answering your calling inspires self-esteem. It is not the accolades of others, but the choice to acknowledge yourself; giving God your "yes" to purpose is a never-ending reward.

## SETTLING VS. SOARING

> "There is no passion to be found playing small - in settling for a life that is less than the one you are capable of living."
> - Nelson Mandela

Settling means that somewhere along the way, we gave up on the life we truly desired and forced ourselves to fit into the one we created. When we forfeit our genuine calling, we find ourselves in the painful cycle of counterfeits, and comparison. We judge the achievements of others. We criticize their projects rather than examine our lack of creative courage. We are more easily led astray by counterfeits and distractions, as scripture states: **Where there is no vision, the people perish. *(Proverbs 29:18)***

In our society, we witness people perishing in fear, addiction, anxiety, and cultural conformity. We live in a culture of envy, apathy and voyeuristic distractions. Judging and comparing ourselves to others is a sure sign that we are not showing up fully and authentically in our own lives. When we are focused on our sacred mission, we don't have the time to look to the left or the right; our eyes remain on our race.

We are also living in the most profound time of purpose, prosperity, and innovation. The time is ripe for the called and chosen to rise.

The calling inspires a mission-mindset, it empowers focus.

When we walk in the authenticity of our calling, we stand alone. There is nothing to compare. Authenticity always stands alone. We can rise above the painful grip of envy and embrace the firm belief that everyone deserves the right to their unique expression in life. There is enough to go around for us all. Compromised self-esteem causes us to shrink in self-imposed limitations rather than expand in our God-given possibilities. The love-led mind believes in abundance and limitless provision. The fear-based mind believes in lack and loss. This world is expansive enough to honor the spirits of countless great thinkers, creators, and visionaries.

When we do what makes us feel joy, what brings our hearts to life, we give this world a gift -- the gift of being open-hearted, fully alive and fully engaged. The calling to purpose is not self-centered; it is always about making a meaningful contribution to the lives of others.

When we pursue God's love, peace, and wholeness, all good things will pursue us. Look within, what do you desire? What parts of your heart have you numbed, killed off, or silenced to prevent future or perceived shame? In what ways have you settled or denied your heart? In what ways have you allowed your decisions to be controlled or managed by cultural, social, religious, or family traditions?

Our souls become exhausted, resisting, and avoiding the truth. When we compromise our truth, we diminish in confidence and self-worth, by betraying our hearts. Our unique gifts will propel us financially to places our fear-based illusions could never imagine. When you work for money, you earn a living; when you walk in your calling, you receive one.

## MIRACLES ARE DISCOVERED A FEW STEPS OUTSIDE OF YOUR COMFORT ZONE

> "The intuitive mind is a sacred gift, and the rational mind is a faithful servant. We have created a society that honors the servant and has forgotten the gift."
> – Albert Einstein

Our hearts will only be denied for so long because our inner voice of Divine intuitive wisdom rings out. The Holy Spirit is prompting us to move forward.

Several years ago, I worked with a client who stepped outside of her familiar world of engineering to launch a successful lingerie company. She answered the call to enter the realm of the unfamiliar. She was willing to risk failure. She was brave, bold, and after her first lingerie event was a tremendous success, she celebrated her decision to choose herself!

Choosing yourself requires a deep trust in the inner voice of God-guided wisdom. New colors, opportunities, challenges, and rewards lay right outside of our realm of comfort. With the limitless possibilities in this world, what makes people choose more of the same? The same jobs? Same relationships? Same neighborhoods? The same seat at their weekly church service? Comfort. When we have compromised self-esteem, we are less likely to venture into the unknown. It requires expanded worth to stretch beyond the borders of our self-inflicted-limitations.

Our uniqueness is what makes us a rare soul, and what makes us unique is our value to the marketplace. Conformity never inspires creativity. Courage is the author of creativity, and courage is the opposite of conformity.

## PLAYING YOUR SACRED ROLE

"For I know the plans I have for you, declares the Lord, plans to prosper you and not to harm you, plans to give you hope and a future."
– Jeremiah 29:11

There is a plan for your life; a predestined course that is set up to reveal *God's Glory* through your calling. You possess a Divine promise. You are neither too late, nor too early.

You are where you are destined to be at this moment, reading these words, reflecting on your next move. God knew before the foundation of time that this moment would arrive.

There is a sacred chain of events interwoven throughout your life. Your life is leading you to a holy encounter with Divine timing, where everything will come together, and it will all make perfect sense.

There is a greater mission at hand. Our role is not only to discover that mission but also to give God our full *yes,* even before *how* is figured out. When we give God our surrendered *yes* to a higher calling, we trust not only in that moment, but in the moments that will unfold over the coming days, weeks, and years. We yield to the process of our unveiling and preparation for a higher purpose.

We are here to play a Sacred role in this world that is ours alone to play.

We do not need to look like, sound like, or create like anyone else. We allow the Master Artist and Creator to move uniquely through us with gifts, creativity, wisdom, strategy, and love.

## FEELING LOST? LET LOVE LEAD

> "I beg you to have patience with everything unresolved in your heart and try to love the questions themselves as if they were locked rooms or books written in a very foreign language. Don't search for the answers which could not be given to you now, because you would not be able to live them. And the point is, to LIVE EVERYTHING. Live the questions now. Perhaps then, someday far in the future, you will gradually, without even noticing it, LIVE your way into the answers."
> – Rainer Maria Rilke

I have met people who have become paralyzed by the purpose-seeking hamster wheel. They drift aimlessly, and often painfully, searching for what is out there that will ignite their passion and cause them to connect with the truth of their calling. The calling is an *inside job*. I believe that we all come to this conclusion in different ways, but we often hide, shrink, and become confused by our obsessive questioning and lack of focus. Indecision and impatience are assassins of the calling.

Those who need to have every question answered before they begin will never begin. Again, clarity reveals itself *as we move*. Having an internal, intuitive guide along the way is priceless. Trying to control the outcome before we even start is our default setting of fear. Life will spring up like fresh rivers to guide us into our calling and help us fulfill our calling. The right people, the right plans, and all the circumstances will line up as we move forward by faith.

God's work is complete. We must do ours. Our job is to give our limitations over to a limitless Creator. Our job is to let our light shine, to dig up the dreams we have buried in our hearts, to unearth the heart-vision hidden beneath the losses, fears, and justifications. Additionally, we must rise above the shadows of what we perceive as a past failure and release the courage to be open to God's restorative grace.

Open-heartedness gives us the courage to believe once more in the beauty of our dreams. Being brave allows us to put our work, book, business idea, screenplay, or product out there; because we desire to live freely and genuinely. Being open-hearted also allows you to *live your way into the answers*, to be at peace with seasons of uncertainty, knowing that real security comes from the vision we hold within.

## CHOSEN TO CREATE

> "Consider the Swiss watchmakers who turned down the technology of the digital watch or the record companies who failed to anticipate the compact disc. Take five minutes and list some assumptions about your children, your spouse, your friends, your relationships, your government, your talents, and your business. Now look them over and decide how many of them are really fact. You may be surprised; you may even feel a little uncomfortable. And if you have come from the mindset that your way is the only way, it may be hard to accept that you might have assumed incorrectly."
> – Peter Drucker

The world has changed. The old, stagnant guard of steadfast tradition and convention has fallen. Those who cling to the former may lack the courage to embrace the new. Now, more than ever, we need people bold enough to innovate, create, and allow themselves the freedom to sit down and do the work of their souls. Doing the work requires us to look from within and design from our personal, God-given genius, not listen to the marketplace and let it dictate what it wants. From this *"seat of genius,"* as author Steven Pressfield calls it, we access our authentic, creative power.

God is the Master Artist moving the world and people through both pain and beauty. The most successful leaders, executives, teachers, parents, chefs, and business people are creative. It takes innovation, vision, and deep original thought to solve the increasing problems of this new millennium workplace.

As the safety of college, career, and traditional roles wane, and the waters of *normal* become cloudier, we must create in sync with the moment. We must evolve. We must leave our imprint on this society. In the end, legacy is all that matters. Creativity requires courage.

We are all creative. Taking ownership of the development of our right (creative) brain is crucial. As Daniel Pink describes in his best-selling book, A Whole New Mind: Why Right-Brainers will Rule the Future: "Lawyers. Accountants. Computer Programmers. That's what our parents encouraged us to become when we grew up. But Mom and Dad were wrong. The future belongs to a very different kind of person with a very different kind of mind. The era of 'left brain' dominance, and the Information Age that it engendered, are giving way to a new world in which 'right brain' qualities- inventiveness, empathy, and meaning predominate."

It is the flexible thinkers, the creative warriors who will design an ideal future in this new world. Many of us have envisioned unique inventions, brilliant stories, amazing product ideas, yet we surrender to the other voice -- fear. We let our most consistent enemy, fear, rob us of our birthright to create and ascend to personal greatness. When we find the courage to not only think outside of the box but never return to it, we rise to the challenge that this world has presented. We can no longer hide and trust that *the powers that be* will decide and dictate our path. We are living in the "Choose Yourself Era" as author James Altucher describes in his lectures and books:

"Because of technology, and the total breaking down of societal, financial, and psychological barriers brought on by the financial catastrophe, it's become more acceptable, even welcome, to CHOOSE YOURSELF. You no longer have to wait for the big media companies to call you. You no longer have to wait for the big companies to reach down from the sky and offer you a job. You build your platform and then select yourself to be the star of it."

The call requires that we choose ourselves, through vision, not the limits of sight. Choosing ourselves requires bravery, humble dependence on God, healthy self-esteem and self-worth. To discover what we love and spend our lives creatively learning how to expand, touch lives, and build wealth from it is a sacred act. To find creative ways to propel us above the shackles of dependency on the old systems of earning money by trading time for hours is an act of wisdom. It's time to choose you.

It takes a creative mind to explore all the possibilities of freedom, expression, and connection this world offers. It takes creativity to make something from an inspirational whisper within your soul to a tangible product or service.

For thousands of years, the power of creativity has fueled the passionate, brilliant hearts of many brave souls. Vision is more potent than reality. A person who walks in their calling will not allow their sight to block vision. Imagination is more powerful than reality. As the cliche states: *Eyes that look are common, but eyes that **see** are rare.* Visionary people see where others look. We are called to create something worthy of us and our legacy. We are called to give God a return on the investment of brilliance, genius, and ingenuity that was infused into our souls before we took our first breath.

You are worthy of creating a life that is an expression of your authentic truth. As we let God lead, we trust that even though we have not figured it all out, God has. The more we nurture healthy self-worth, the more comfortable we find it to trust our calling. Love will lead us to the truth, higher destiny, and life that transcends all limits. It's time to "**walk worthy of your calling." (Ephesians 4:1)**

## A WORTHY Belief

"Discovering and walking in your God-given calling is the highest work of your soul. Walking in your calling is the pathway to genuine fulfillment and a great life."

## **WORTHY Key Takeaways:**

1. Answering our calling is our most magnificent journey, the one that leads us back home to the truth of who we are.
2. Scores of us talk ourselves out of a new idea by over-thinking into the future.
3. Refusing to accept anything less than God created us to be is the best form of rebellion.
4. The force of resistance attempts to do one thing: stop us from doing our work.
5. Your life's calling is the answer to someone's prayer. It is your unique contribution to this world.
6. A called life requires that we first surrender our default beliefs and open our hearts to receive the abundant provisions God has in store.
7. It is not the accolades of others; it is the choice to acknowledge yourself, choose yourself, and answer your God-given calling that is the highest reward.
8. When we walk in the authenticity of our call, we stand - alone. There is nothing to compare. Authenticity always stands alone.
9. When you work for money, you earn a living; when you walk in your calling, you receive one.
10. Choosing yourself requires deep trust in the inner voice of intuitive, God-given wisdom.
11. It takes innovation, vision, and in-depth creative thought to solve the increasing problems of this new millennium workplace.
12. Many of us have envisioned products to invent, stories to write, movie scripts to pound out, yet we surrender to the voice of fear-based resistance.
13. We are called to leave our authentic imprint on this world. It's our legacy. We are called to leave this world a better place. We are called to create something **worthy** of us.

**WORTHY Soul Reflection Questions:**

1. What can you do this week to step outside of your comfort zone and begin creating a new life?

2. How has a fear of finances or *not being good enough* caused you to settle for jobs/careers not aligned with your purpose? How will you begin to change this?

3. What parts of your heart have you numbed, killed off, or silenced to prevent future perceived hurt or failure? How will you heal this?

4. In what ways have you settled or lied to yourself to stay within your comfort zone? What will you do to change this?

5. In what ways have you allowed your decisions to be controlled or managed by cultural, social expectations, religious or family traditions? How will you expand beyond these limits?

**WORTHY Affirmation:**

"I was created for such a time as this. I will walk in the boldness and power of my God-given calling. I will not shrink back or hide my truth. I will rise daily to the occasion of my greatness."

# Key Eight: Complete

> "Looking back, you realize that a very special person passed briefly through your life and that person was you. It is not too late to become that person again."
> – Robert Brault

Webster's Dictionary defines complete to mean: "Not lacking anything, not limited in any way." Freedom belongs to the person who has nothing left to prove. What you think you lack, you already own.

We live in a world that cultivates deception and disconnection from God and self. A culture that bombards us with constant temptations to look outside of ourselves for our value. We are already complete. God-centered-self-worth is a connector; it creates a harmony of mind, body, spirit.

There is nothing that we lack when we look to, lean on, and trust God's Infinite wisdom. "The kingdom is within."

Although we acknowledge our worthiness, it doesn't mean we stop cultivating, expanding, evolving, and unveiling our worth.

Seasons of hardships, heartbreak, and loss have a way of making us forget our value. Many of us have already lived through a *dark night of the soul*.

This wilderness season is also necessary for our growth. Because of our human conditioning, we tend to forget that even in times of pain, we are healing, growing, and deepening in wisdom.

## DYING TO THE FORMER SMALL LIFE, SOARING TO NEW HEIGHTS

> "You must want to be a butterfly so badly; you are willing to give up being a caterpillar."
> – Sekou Andrews

On the journey of wholeness and completion, we will enter the dark places, a cocoon-like state, not designed to destroy us, but to engineer a higher view of life, God and self.

You have risen above the lesser things and soared into a greater understanding; you are evolving into a deeper spiritual maturity.

Pain and setbacks in life will still happen; yet, you will have an inner-compass of faith that guides you back home to the peace of God within. By faith, you refuse to allow yourself to slip into former habits, mentalities, and energies that bind you and rob you of energy through unnecessary struggle and suffering.

## THE BEAUTIFUL PAIN OF GROWTH

> "The lotus is the most beautiful flower whose petals open one by one. But it will only grow in the mud. In order to grow and gain wisdom, first, you must have the mud --- the obstacles of life and its suffering ... The mud speaks of the common ground that humans share, no matter what our stations in life ... Whether we have it all or we have nothing, we are all faced with the same obstacles: sadness, loss, illness, dying, and death. If we are to strive as human beings to gain more wisdom, more kindness, and more compassion, we must have the intention to grow as a lotus and open each petal one by one."
> – Goldie Hawn

When a patient is ill, a doctor will take them through a course of treatments and medical protocols. These treatments may not feel good; however, the end goal in mind is healing. When we sign up for the journey of conscious growth, we permit the Divine Physician to lead us through the best course of healing protocols possible. The spiritual treatments may hurt, wound, or crush temporarily; yet, ultimately, we are rising higher into a space of unsurpassable peace and joy. It is what we term the low places that deepen our wisdom to sustain the significant and higher opportunities for which we are trusting. Scripture states that **"no discipline seems pleasant at the time, but in the end, it produces a harvest of righteousness." (Hebrews 12:11)**

What may feel like it is killing us, is by God's grace, rebirthing us. What feels like is crushing us, is purifying us. The "valley" moments are not times to lose hope, but to increase in the stamina of our faith and the strength of our character.

As we mature, we learn to embrace our seasons of darkness as quickly as we do our seasons of light. All humanity will face obstacles to test and prove their resilience. The temptation during difficult times is to fall back into demanding the outcome that happens our way and our timeline. Impatience is rooted in the fear that our needs will not be met. But God does not forget His promises, and we as scripture states: **"Hold steadfast to the profession of our faith without wavering because the God who promised is faithful. (Hebrews 10:23)** Nobody likes waiting. Few of us welcome the pain or unsettling feeling of uncertainty. Yet, as we are waiting, God is changing us. When our prayers do not change the situation, it means the situation is challenging us to change.

Delay does mean denial, it usually means something needs our attention. Patience is a spiritual gift that anchors and calms the soul as we are being prepared for the promise. We can learn as we mature to embrace the process of waiting, not as pain, but as grace. God knows the exact moment and time of our breakthrough, our complaining won't advance our cause, our diligent preparation will. God's timing is always perfect and we don't have to like it or trust it, it's just easier if we do.

We can relax, allow, and receive. We can deepen our resilience and allow God's glorious inner-peace to cultivate us during times of transition. There is a matchless beauty on the other side of the struggle. A stunning unfolding of our petals, we will rise above the muck and muddiness like the lotus. We will awaken and expand in new clarity and light. We will come out sooner than we think, and our lives will reveal a masterpiece of the soul. Our lives will reflect a depth, refinement, and strength that could have only developed in the darkrooms of life.

## THERE IS A MESSAGE IN YOUR MESS

> "My brethren, count it all joy when you fall into various trials, knowing that the testing of your faith produces patience. But let patience have its perfect work, that you may be perfect and complete, lacking nothing."
> – James 1:2-4 (NKJV)

If it's hard, it's teaching you. If it's tough, it's stretching you. If it's painful, it's purifying you. If it's delayed, it's disciplining you. No matter what "it" is, in the end, you'll be better, wiser, more prosperous, and stronger for it.

These soul lessons may be painful to our human experience. On the interior of our being, they accomplish what the truer longing of our soul required, wisdom. Wisdom provides beauty, blessings, and honor long after the hardship passes. We remain in the pain only as long as we lack the understanding that the trial is here to provide. When we receive the wisdom, the suffering ceases. What feels like it's killing us is completing our wholeness through faith.

What we may perceive as a loss is a more profound gain. We gain our self-respect for rising whole and confident over what we thought would destroy us. In retrospect, we acknowledge that adversity helped define and refine us. Instead of asking God, why me? We learn to ask, what's next? We look for the seed of opportunity contained within the obstacle. We gain endurance and peace as we realize the disharmony of roadblocks and challenges also provide the sweet melody of our redemption song.

We increase our resilience and bravery because we don't run or hide from the pain. We cultivate the inner knowing that our promise is near. We speak, visualize, and declare it by faith. We courageously surrender the questions of *how* and *when* to a God whose timing is always perfectly aligned with the higher strategy and destiny for our lives. We find the courage to live in the now. We bring our best and highest work and focus to the sacredness of the present moment.

We acknowledge compassionately to ourselves that this period of life is tough, but we don't quit on God, the people we love, our vision, or ourselves. When we emerge from our dark night, our season of trials or adversity, we substantially overcome the lies of this world to become our true selves.

This season of waiting is one that purchases our growth, our spiritual and emotional intelligence. Entering the season of trial by fire accelerates our spiritual wholeness. Despise not the dark night of the soul. Once we press through, we transcend the former life, the previous struggles, the old self, and we are reborn into a new identity. We are free.

I would not trade my seasons of suffering for anything. What I considered my painful times purchased something in my heart more profound than I have yet found the words to articulate. The rainbow only appears after the storm. The deepness of the soul often matches the deepness of the trial. The greatest souls have suffered much.

Pain is a teacher. Suffering is a sage. The wisdom of both contains seeds of opportunity. These emotional states help us to identify any belief system that would keep us from our natural state of wholeness and inner radiance. We do not have to learn every lesson through the pain. We can learn lessons in inspiration and joy. No matter what it looks or feels like in this present moment, we can trust that just as sure as the air we breathe, God's promise will not fail, and neither will we.

## PREPARATION ACCELERATES THE PROMISE

"The secret of success in life is for a man to be ready for his opportunity when it comes."
– Benjamin Disraeli

Every moment of pain is attached to a more significant promise. Every promise requires our preparation. To understand our worthiness is also to realize that God has a plan, even during the temporary discomfort. The hardship is being used for us, not against us. No matter what it feels like, all things are working together for our good. Change the lens in which you see life and the life you see will change.

We often become so obsessed with the big door opening that we neglect the subtle needs around us. God's timing is perfect. There is an intensity of joy that increases with anticipation. Faith-based expectancy adds life and happiness. We are called in scripture to **"Call the things that are not as though they were." (Romans 4:17)** Even if it looks hopelessly dead, we embody through our Risen Savior the authority to speak and flow in resurrection power.

Nothing is impossible with God. Worry and impatience deplete and distract our energy and focus. We take the limits off of self by renewing our faith in God.

We must learn to prepare while we wait. We can learn to see delays as a sign that something in our private world needs ordering. Private order sustains public success. There is a season of private editing of one's life that proceeds public promotion. This sacred process requires patience. As one of my spiritual mentors used to say: *Patience is the weapon that forces deceit to reveal itself.* You are neither too late or too early. All things are aligning with God's Divine time and destiny for your life.

We often seek and obsess over what we cannot control rather than pay attention to the simple things in our lives that we can. As we mature, we understand that it is the preparation that expands our capacity for success; it is faith in motion.

Rather than inflict pain upon ourselves by stressing over false control, we can engage in life with simplicity and action. We can clean and organize our homes, start an exercise class, change our eating habits, increase our water intake, expand our knowledge through inspirational books, and reading the Word of God, we can serve our community or focus deeper on healing within our immediate family. We can allow our faith to prove itself through daily action. We can draw closer to God. We can devote more time and focus to nurturing ourselves and our Body Temples. Worrying, and a *defeated attitude while waiting* evokes powerlessness and pain. We often get angry with God for not delivering big blessings that we have not adequately prepared to receive. Waiting becomes a powerful advancement when coupled with preparation and strategy to impact and improve what we can, using what we have.

The movement towards bettering our immediate environment or ourselves serves to increase our capacity to win when it is due time. Due time always arrives, *often sooner than we think*. The question is: "Will you be prepared?"

## THE COMPLETION OF VOLUNTARY DEATH

"If you cling to your life, you will lose it, and if you let your life go, you will save it."
– Luke 17:33

In our grasping, longing, and yearning, we have not reached a place of completion. Completion is the acknowledgment that the rainbows we seek outside of ourselves are within. We will access the courage to allow life to unfold in perfect order. The spiritual poise that I now possess is the Divine contentment that comes from trust. There is a remarkable anointing of grace and ease that floods your life when you choose to allow, trust, and receive, rather than fearfully grasp and attempt to control the outcome.

We often want to engage life on our terms instead of trusting the highest way for our souls. The highest path for our lives is the Kingdom's promise of love, peace, and joy. We can release false attachments to the trappings of this world and inwardly receive the keys to lasting peace. Detachment doesn't mean you will live in poverty, owning nothing; it means you rise with real wealth because nothing owns you.

When we give up our demanding, begging, groveling, cajoling, and treating God like a white-bearded magician, who answers at our entitled beck and call, we begin to move through life with more exceptional spiritual elegance and faith anchored patience. Detachment is making room, trusting the timing, process, and sacred journey of our unfolding and destiny.

If you are forcing or fighting to hold on to something you feel you need to possess, it has come to *possess you*. Detachment creates peace. It is in the surrendered state that our soul becomes luminous, flooded with the light of relaxed magnetism.

Nothing or no one can derail your destiny. You don't have to force anything. Relax. Allow. Receive. You've chased, you've hustled, and you've strived. Now exhale. Trust. Give it over to God. Let it come to you. We often exhaust ourselves trying to force something that will come effortlessly at the right time and in the proper season.

As we increase in wholeness, we learn to trust the possibilities of Source over the limitations of self.

## THE FOCUSED COMPLETION OF YOUR ASSIGNMENTS

"The end of a matter is better than its beginning, and patience is better than pride."
– Ecclesiastes 7:8

As much as I love living and operating in the higher elevations of the spirit realm, you would not be reading this book right now if I did not intentionally engage focused action and daily discipline in the earth realm. Completion is a God-like discipline. God creates.

God completes. Achievement of our work, our goals, visions, and ideas, aligns us with the same powerful co-creative energy that hung the stars in the galaxy. Pride is impatient. Pride demands that things be done on it's terms and timeline; humility patiently accepts, allows and makes room for God's best.

The spiritual position of humility provides the patience to stay the course. Humility empowers us to tap into Divine resources, strategy and wisdom as we grow in deeper dependency on God.

Completion is our birthright; it is how we move forward, higher, it is how we increase in self-respect. In your quiet time, ask God's Holy Spirit to reveal to you what you need to complete. Open your heart and receive wisdom and direction guided by the Spirit. God will give you strength today and increase your hope for tomorrow. Great is God's faithfulness. Every morning we are met with new mercies. Refuse to allow an undisciplined or prideful mind rob you of the prosperity and peace of completion.

## COMPLETION AND FORGIVENESS

"Inner-peace can be reached only when we practice forgiveness. Forgiveness is letting go of the past, and is, therefore, the means for correcting our misperceptions".
— Gerald G. Jampolsky

The process of God's wholeness is one of liberating us from the shackles of our own doing. We will not experience this level of completion without forgiveness. To live in the past is to live in denial of the power of our present reality. To replay injuries of the past is to prolong suffering. Inner peace is achieved through the daily spiritual practice of emotional cleansing and living in the receptivity of grace.

If you have ever entered someone's home, a person who would be termed a hoarder, you may have found it hard to relax, hard to breathe, and difficult to focus or concentrate.

We have made famous the phrase "Cleanliness is next to Godliness," because we intuitively know that physical objects carry energetic weight. You can become fatigued and overwhelmed, just entering a room crowded with too much clutter. We also experience this lack of peace when our lives are smothered with past offenses. Our painful memories are energy, and the more we hold on to them, the more cumbersome and exhausting life becomes.

Forgiveness is a radical act of self-love and self-compassion; it is an intentional act of self-nurturing. Self-care and self-love are not optional; they are necessities of survival.

We have limited emotional energy. Forgiveness frees up the energetic space we need to create, heal, and flourish. The choice to forgive and release old offenses is the choice to reclaim ownership over your joy. If an ancient offense has its claws in our soul, we are not complete. We are divided, fractured from our wholeness when we refuse to let go.

## SUFFERING IS ONLY HERE TO SERVE THE COMPLETION PROCESS

> "Suffering is an indication that the individual is out of harmony with himself. The supreme use of suffering is to purify, to burn out all that is useless and impure. Suffering ceases for him who is pure. There could be no object in burning gold after the dross had been removed, and a perfectly pure and enlightened being could not suffer."
>
> – James Allen

Many of us have fallen into the false habit of creating suffering for ourselves. We over-think, over-analyze, and allow our unchecked thought life to create suffering. The highest purpose of pain is to identify disease, disharmony, and to drive out anything that is no longer needed. The use of suffering is to bring us to a place where we surrender to the higher truth of a living God.

The people in our lives are mirrors and teachers, revealing what is needed to release, rework, or reset our belief systems.

Love does not mean we open ourselves for others to hurt us. It means we end our suffering by refusing to keep re-injuring ourselves. Love is the greatest liberator, and when unconditional love begins, pain ceases.

## WHOLE. COMPLETE. NOTHING LEFT TO PROVE

> "Consider it pure joy, my brothers and sisters, whenever you face trials of many kinds because you know that the testing of your faith produces perseverance. Let perseverance finish its work so that you may be mature and complete, not lacking anything."
> - James 1:2-4

The trial provides. Through seeking God's presence in the hardship, we gain the wisdom needed to live with peace, completion, and wholeness.

It is about waking up and remembering who we are. We are already enough. We don't strive before God to *earn* our worth; we live from the humble anchoring *of* our God-given worth. The acceptance of our God-given value will strengthen us to remove our grave clothes. The outer layers of deadness and disappointment can be relinquished as we embrace God's gracious and glorious view of our identity.

Joy increases in a heart that is no longer clouded by yesterday's pain or tomorrow's worries. It takes God-confidence to show up in your authentic truth and to shine your light fearlessly, liberating others to do the same. Self-esteem and healthy self-worth are built brick by brick, choice by choice, thought by thought. We don't go instantly from A-Z. We grow daily into the person God predestined us to become.

We may speak **Worthy** long before we are fully convinced of it, or wholeheartedly living it. As human beings, our nature is to reject anything that seems too good to be true. When God is our Source, nothing is too good to be true. We forget that God looks beyond the flaws and sees the need for our souls. Everything our Creator breathes life into is good and longs to reveal its glory. As scripture states: ***"All of creation waits in eager expectation for the children of God to be revealed."*** (Romans 8:19)

When we rise, remember and seek the Source of our worth and value like the prodigal son, heaven, and earth rejoice. Like the prodigal son, even now, God is lovingly and patiently awaiting our return.

God views us through the eyes of completion and joy. Our Creator smiles as we unveil the fullness of our potential, uniqueness, and value as gifts to this world.

You will manifest a life that mirrors your deepest desires and dreams. Worthiness will empower you to evolve daily in self-mastery and personal wholeness. Embracing your worth is an act of faith, humility, and bravery. Refusing to shrink into the shadows of life honors the gifts God desires to reveal through your life. Living with a goal of authentic joy and peace is a confirmation of self-love.

Worthiness expands your capacity to both give and receive love. Essentially, worthiness is taking the journey back home to the truth of who you already are. *Whole. Complete. Lacking nothing.*

## WORTHY.

### A WORTHY Belief

**Each lesson in life is necessary to guide and honor our soul's journey of completion. To be complete means to be enveloped in the unconditional love and peace of our Creator.**

## WORTHY Key Factor Takeaways:

1. The completion process is Divinely guided to bring us into our highest good.
2. We are already complete. There is nothing that we lack when we look to, lean on and
3. trust the infinite wisdom contained within.
4. Timing is, was, and forever shall be everything. We are not waiting; we are being
5. prepared for the promise.
6. 4.     We are called to walk before God as "perfect." Perfection does not mean we live perfectly or "mistake-free." It means we live in a state of completion by God's love.
7. There is wholeness in life: dark and light; life and death; pain and joy. God is a master of justice, balance, and wholeness.
8. Pain is a teacher; suffering is a sage. The wisdom of both contain seeds of opportunity. These emotional states help us to identify any belief system that would keep us from our natural state of wholeness, peace, clarity, and joy.
9. When you own your story, your story will no longer own you.
10. As much as the season of our dark night may hurt us, our soul has ordered the lesson, the more profound healing, and advancement.
11. You are whole. You are complete. You are loved. You are valuable. You are chosen. You are royal. You are precious. You are worthy.
12. Joy increases in a heart that is no longer clouded by yesterday's pain or tomorrow's worries.
13. Circumstances and situations are aligning moment by moment to mirror back to us what we believe.
14. We will soon arrive at a new place of freedom where we can thank God for the valleys in life as much as for our mountain top moments. In the valley, the character is made secure. Courage is released.
15. Forgiveness is a radical act of self-love and self-compassion; it is an intentional act of self-care.

16. Living with a goal of authentic happiness is a confirmation of inner-holiness and self-love.

**WORTHY Soul Reflection Questions:**

1. In what ways have you looked for wholeness, validation, and completion outside of yourself? How will you change this?

2. How will you start cultivating your worthiness through daily action and discipline?

3. What projects, goals, or desires are incomplete in your life? What is your commitment to focus and complete unfinished work?

4. What has been one of the greatest lessons you learned through pain? How did this lesson help to elevate and expand your life?

5. How can you learn to trust and relax during seasons of transitions and challenges?

## WORTHY Affirmation:

"I am whole. I am complete. I lack nothing. I have a depth of wisdom, peace, and understanding within, I am never without anything that I need, and I rest in this truth."

**LET'S STAY CONNECTED ON THE WORTHY JOURNEY!**

We are honored to bring this message of wholeness and healing to the world through a faith-centered message of healthy worth and self-esteem.

Visit www.theworthyvision.com and become a part of our global, thriving vision.

*Find out about our free, LIVE weekly group coaching through our online **Worthy** Tribe, or start your own home-based **Worthy** small group.

*Discover how to receive private coaching through our **Worthy** Coaching Method (™) and ***The Worthy Healing School.***

*Receive mastery-level-coaching certification through in the **Worthy** Coaching Method (™)

## THE WAY THE TRUTH AND THE LIGHT OF WORTHINESS:

Without a personal relationship with our Lord and Savior Jesus Christ, the message of WORTHY will carry no eternal or lasting impact. It is through the exchange of the former life that we position ourselves to inherit the promise.

If you have never invited Jesus Christ into your life to be your personal Lord and Savior, you are WORTHY of the gift of grace, unconditional love and redemption; God is here now.

Please **repeat this simple prayer below:**

*"Dear God, I want to be a part of your Kingdom family. You said in Your Word that if I acknowledge that You raised Jesus from the dead and that I accept Him as my Lord and Savior, I would be saved. So God, I now say that I believe You raised Jesus from the dead and that He is alive and I invite him into my heart, and I accept Him now as my personal Lord and Savior. I repent from my past sin and receive my salvation right now.*

*I confess that Jesus is my Lord. Jesus is my Savior. Thank you, God, for forgiving me, loving me, and giving me eternal life with You. In Jesus name, Amen!"*

If this was your first time saying this prayer, **welcome home!**

I invite you to go back and read **Worthy** again, with new vision and understanding.

Congratulations on your NEW beginning! You are worthy of ALL God has declared about your Destiny. Don't go it alone, visit www.theworthyvision.com and connect with us!

I celebrate and acknowledge your courage and cannot wait to see you in one of our thriving online or off-line *Worthy* communities soon!

*Blessings and love,*

Shannon Evette

Printed by Amazon Italia Logistica S.r.l.
Torrazza Piemonte (TO), Italy

50532057R00106